Revolutionize Your Relationships

Communication Secrets on How to Succeed at Work and at Home

TODD REED, CPC

DEDICATION

I dedicate this book to all the men and women I've had the honor to coach, either face-to-face or through my writing. Watching your confidence soar as your relationships grow and prosper continues to be rewarding beyond words.

CONTENTS

ACKNOWLEDGMENTS

The journey leading to the culmination of this book has been touched by family, friends and those who have been moved by its message. There have been so many influences in my life, and to each person who has placed his/her fingertips on this project, I say, "thank you."

The two most influential people in my life have been my mom and dad. They dedicated their lives to raising a family of four boys and one girl. Not only did they teach all of us the value of unconditional love, they encouraged us to pursue our passions, to always try and make those around us smile and to never pass up the opportunity to make a difference in someone's life. My mom encouraged the creative side of me and told me to always keep dreaming. From my starring role in a high school play to my career as a television broadcaster, I enjoyed sharing those successes with her. When it came to my dad, there's only one word I could ever use to describe him: Hero. He was larger than life to all of us and influenced each of us in his own way. He was an amazing athlete in his day and taught all of his sons to play and enjoy the game of golf. He played with some of the game's legends, and even though he has passed, I look forward to the day that we can stand on the first tee and swing away one more time.

There's no question that I wouldn't be where I am today if not for my brother, Tim. We always joke and tell people that we are really twins that were born six years apart. No words can describe the bond we have and how much we mean to each other. He's the funniest person I've ever met in my life, and he's always been there for me in both good times and bad. I'm proud to be his "little" brother.

My oldest brother, Tom, has always been the statesman of our family and carried the torch of being the senior sibling in an amazing fashion. The love he has for each one of us is incredible, and while he did once beat me in a one-on-one game of basketball (which he never lets me forget), I still love him.

My brother, Ted, has entertained us for years on the golf course. When asked what type of golf ball he prefers to play with, he simply responds, "The ones that say 'Range' on them," as in the range balls you hit at the course to get warmed up. He never could bring himself to buy those expensive balls that come in a package. Surprisingly, Titleist has never offered him a contract.

And then there's my little sister, Tevi, whom I love with all my heart...partially because she has more "dirt" on me than anybody else. We were only two years apart, and needless to say, I did some very embarrassing things in my youth. Guess who was right there watching and remembering every single incident?

The sparkle in my eye comes from my daughter, Raquel, who warms my heart with every word, sound and touch. I'll never forget the first time I held her in my arms. Even though she refuses to stay young and not grow up, I'll never forget rocking her to sleep each night, watching her figure out how to roll over, then take her first step and listen to her say her prayers at night while sucking her thumb. She's an amazing young lady, and I love her so much.

Being in love feels great, but finding the love of your life is "magical." Sherry and I have a connection that amazes me to this day. The way she makes me feel, the way she looks at me and how she takes care of me is indescribable. She allows me to breathe, and like a fresh spring breeze, always makes me feel alive and refreshed.

When it comes to the colleagues that helped put my career and this project together, I simply have two of the best. If not for Barbara Smalley, you wouldn't be reading this book or have even heard about me. Her commitment and passion for our message is awe-inspiring. I nicknamed her "The Bulldozer," because when she believes in something—or in this case, someone—nothing will stand in her way of sharing that cause or person with the rest of the world. What started as a business relationship has grown much bigger and deeper; she's simply family now and a huge part of making this project happen. And I have to give a shout out to my other colleague, Cliff Armstrong. Cliff was there when I wrote my first book and has been a major player in the process ever since. Having worked with and traveled the world with one of the industry's greats, Tony Robbins, Cliff's advice, feedback and desire to affect people's lives has proven invaluable.

A special "thanks" goes to my brother-from-another-mother, Bob Veroulis. For 20 years, Bobby and I have shared some amazing times in both Montana and California. As a PGA teaching professional, he and I have created a million memories while playing golf, but his most valuable contribution to me has been his incredible friendship. He's supported me, counseled me and always encouraged me to have faith and continue to look up and never give up—no matter how tough things got. He's one of the most amazing people I've ever known, and I'm honored to call him my "brother."

To my adopted family, The Sheridans, in Arlee Montana at the S4 Ranch: Barney, Tara, Cody and Nikki. Somewhere along the way you all became family and let me become a part of yours. The support and friendship we share is incredibly special to me, and I apologize for Cody and I driving you crazy playing video games all night. Oh, and I don't ever want to see the huge Black Bear on your back porch again...lol. You guys make Big Sky Country a special place...and "Go Griz!"

They say friendship can stand the test of time, and Scott Magerer has proven that to be fact. We first met back in the mid 1980s when he taught me how to be a nightclub DJ. We formed a great friendship back then, and it continues to this day. He went on to build his small company into a large entertainment business that I'm proud to have been a part of. Add another "brother" to my list of siblings. Finally, I have to give a special thanks to my man, Moeid Mohammad, who has supported us and unselfishly offered his time to move the process forward...he's a great friend.

Last, but far from least, I am deeply grateful to the men and women I've had the honor to coach and to the hundreds of couples who have gotten in touch (via email, phone and letters) to tell me how much my teachings have benefitted their relationships. Your feedback is what keeps me passionate about what I do. Keep it coming!

- *Coach Todd Reed*

INTRODUCTION

As an author and a speaker I'm often asked, "Why do you do what you do?" The following story will answer that very question and prove that, as a man, I not only embrace my masculinity, I also understand that as a man, it's o.k. to experience emotional vulnerability.

One of the highlights of my life was the day my daughter entered this world. Being the first person to ever feed her, holding her in my arms was both amazing and intimidating. She was totally dependent on her mother and me to feed her, bathe her and take care of her. As a first time parent, I worried that I was going to do something wrong and that the results of those actions would be everlasting.

Over the next three years, I experienced the highs and lows that come with being a parent. No greater memories stand out than those of my infant daughter falling asleep on my chest after eating her dinner, feeling the warmth of her little body, glancing down and seeing the cutest look on her face or rocking her to sleep before placing her in her crib for the night. It's funny how, years later, I don't seem to remember the piercing sound of her crying for long periods of time, the sleepless nights or the many illnesses that little kids experience. No, it's the sweet and tender moments that fill my memory bank.

What I *do* remember with crystal-clear clarity, however, is the day I had to force myself to keep pushing down on the accelerator of my truck as it climbed the ramp connected to the interstate and the gut-wrenching pain that was tearing me apart as I merged on to the highway and began heading south. My marriage had failed, and I knew that I would never be the dad I'd always wanted to be...the same kind of dad that I was so fortunate to be blessed with growing up. Like accidentally burning yourself on an open flame or a pan you just retrieved from the oven, my heart burned with a sadness I'd never experienced before.

As the reality of my situation began to sink in, uncontrollable tears began running down my face. My eyes gazed at the road ahead, but all I could see was my daughter's face in the reflection of my windshield. With each passing second, the internal pain seemed only to intensify, the tears kept coming and my mind was racing with a myriad of thoughts that I had no chance of either catching or sorting through. I was flashing back to the day she first rolled over, the day she first crawled and the day she first walked. And possibly the most gut wrenching thoughts going through my head were: "Will she remember me?" and "What kind of impact will I ever really have on her life?" The upper part of my shirt was soaked, as if I'd just worked out at the gym. But it was wet with tears, not sweat. I could barely function or focus on the road. There was no question that, along with the passing of my dad, this was the worst day of my life. It took months for me to even begin to come to terms with the situation, and to this day, I still experience the emotional fallout from my marital relationship not working out.

It wasn't long after that day that I committed myself to helping people become better communicators and to avoid feeling the kind of pain I felt on that cold winter day. Reflecting on my twelve years of marriage, I spent a great deal of time soul searching and realizing that even though it wasn't obvious to me then, there were very specific situations where I didn't possess the skills to navigate my relationship successfully. For instance, I often avoided confrontation, and when I felt my needs weren't getting met, I didn't speak up.

This book is dedicated to explaining the importance of communication, both verbal and non-verbal, and explaining how and why people need strong communication skills to survive...and to thrive. Communication is the *number one* factor that determines the success of work and personal relationships. Smartphones, tablets and the increasing demands placed on both our personal and professional lives are eating away at not only our overall communication skills but also our desire to improve these vital skills.

Modern technology has clearly affected how we communicate both at home and at work. With so many high-tech gadgets at our fingertips, the demands on our time and attention only seem to multiply—not to mention the impact these devices have on our relationships. Not surprisingly, research reveals that many of us spend more time texting, emailing, chatting on Facebook and instant messaging each other than we do actually *talking* to one another. In fact, according to the most recent data, Americans send/receive over 184 *billion* text messages each month! Think about what happens every time you receive a text message. Not only does it interrupt your brain function and attention, it directs your focus away from the people or tasks you're experiencing at the moment.

This is not to say that high-tech devices don't come in handy...I use them all the time. But the more people rely on technology to communicate, the more they start to drift apart. In other words, if we're not careful, these devices can quickly rob us of meaningful dialogue and face-to-face communication.

I recently received an email from a couple asking me to help them restore the communication and the connectivity in their marriage. Life, work, the kids and technology had played a role in eroding the foundation of their relationship. I helped them create a schedule that allowed them to get back to communicating the "old-fashioned" way. The end result was that, as a couple and a family, they quickly began to grow closer and started having way more fun.

The better able you are to communicate with others, the happier and more successful you will be in *all* arenas of your life. Rewarding and lucrative careers, strong and lasting friendships, meaningful and satisfying romance all hang on this one uniquely human ability. It never ceases to amaze me that when I observe or hear about people that are struggling at work, home or with their friendships, inevitably, the problem relates to communication. They're either not feeling heard/understood, or they're not listening or verbalizing their thoughts in an effective manner. This book delves deep into exposing what it takes to become an effective communicator. *Revolutionize Your Relationships* is all about giving you the tools, tips and techniques that will allow you to be successful with whomever you speak too.

Given the changing societal climate, it should come as no surprise that communication skills are highly sought after by employers and are a major factor in determining whether personal/romantic relationships succeed or fail. I've accumulated over 20 years of communication, relationship and coaching experience that has allowed me to help individuals and couples—

both nationally and internationally—become better and more effective communicators. In the coming chapters you'll hear real-life stories from those who've been able to reconnect at home and/or at work and are now maximizing their professional and personal lives. In some cases, the men and women I've coached have come to realize how changing even *just one* communication habit can quickly transform your quality of life, both professionally and personally.

Chapter One

FROM STONE AGE TO NEW AGE

Imagine having a conversation with your significant other that goes something like this:

> **Man:** *"Me head out to forest with other men to hunt for food. You stay here to watch over cave and little one. I be back before sundown."*

> **Woman:** *"Bring back good meat for us to cook. I use feather duster to clean home and prepare for your return."*

Okay, so maybe feather dusters didn't exist in the Stone Age, but conversation, even though it was primitive, certainly did. Over time, the way men and women communicate with each other has definitely evolved. To understand the modern-day dynamic between the two sexes, it only seems logical to call on the greatest teaching tool we have: history. I've always been a history buff and have learned over the years that the answers to so many of our questions lie with those who have blazed the trail before us. While the image of Fred Flintstone arriving home after a long day at the quarry with his pal Barney Rubble, then walking through the front door and yelling "Wilma, I'm home...what's for dinner?" may have fit a generation of quite some years ago, it's just as likely today that Wilma would be the one arriving home after an exhausting day at work and yelling, "Fred, I'm home...what's for dinner?"

So how did we get from there to here? How have the ways in which men and women communicate evolved? And how has it changed the dynamic in the relationships we have? Let's start with a trip back in time...

Is it really all that crazy to think that, once upon a time, not only did men and women work well together, but that the two sexes actually communicated effectively and got along with relative ease? Their roles were clearly defined: Men were responsible for hunting, protecting the village and being good problem solvers. Women were in charge of the cave and looked after the children. Not only did this structure work, it worked effectively. Men became expert hunters, developing a keen sense of direction. And as protectors, they would give their lives in order to keep their families safe. Meanwhile, women focused on keeping the home fires burning and mastered reading the signs of behavioral changes in children and adults, developed short-range navigational skills and honed a keen sense of detecting danger. Communication between the sexes could mostly be described as harmonious, mostly because there was a mutual understanding of what each person was in charge of. In other words, gender roles and responsibilities were clear.

As they evolved, men and women adapted physically to the roles that defined them. Men became stronger, faster and their brains developed to suit their tasks. Women were content with their men working away from home, and their brains developed to cope with their responsibilities of keeping their homes running smoothly. The two sexes continued to operate under these guidelines for thousands of years, but I'm sure you've already begun thinking about how much different life is now compared to the Stone Age. "Me cave man, you cave woman" doesn't compute in today's world. Not even close. Over the last 100 million-plus years, we have undergone huge changes in both the workplace and at home.

When A Woman's Place Was (Mostly) In The Home

In the early 1900s, only one out of every five women worked for wages (the role of homemaker was not factored into labor statistics at that time), with the highest percentage working in factory and service jobs (as hotel maids, laundry workers and the like). The typical working female was single and worked to support herself or her family. In fact, only one out of every twenty married women worked, and those that did mainly took jobs to support their families. Meanwhile, nine of ten men in their early twenties were landing jobs and beginning careers. While the days of chasing woolly mammoths had long passed, the family structure of the man heading off to work and the woman staying at home to be the child bearer and keep the home fires burning was the norm. That being the case, the channels of communication were still very much the same as they had been—with both sexes respecting the other's role as they continued to build a life together. While change was on the horizon, this family unit remained rock solid, as husband and wife continued to complement one another.

By 1910, the number of married women punching clocks had risen from five to eleven percent. As for the unattached, no longer was every woman's goal to marry, have children and obey her husband. Many yearned for higher education and a meaningful career. Support for these lofty goals came from the growing Women's Suffrage Movement, which had its heyday from about 1910 to 1914, culminating in the passage of the 19th Amendment in 1920. Yet, all the while, psychologists and anti-suffragists chastised career-minded women for "rocking the boat." Feminists, they argued, were mentally unstable and could not be taken seriously. Moreover, allowing women to vote would not only jeopardize the country's security, but also make women more masculine and the men who allowed them to vote more effeminate. Seriously?

Enter The Roaring Twenties

Most people associate the 1920s with "flappers"... rebellious women who bobbed their hair, wore short skirts, smoked cigarettes, drank gin (despite Prohibition) and flaunted their sexuality by dancing the night away in speakeasies. But the media of this decade depicted the majority of women as happy homemakers. Nevertheless, as cities and suburbs began to take shape, the influx of middle-class women into the workforce gained momentum. In fact, during the first thirty years of the 20th century, the ranks of married women entering the workforce doubled. For the first time in history, we began to see a noticeable rise in the number of "dual income families." Better educated than earlier generations and now armed with legal power, women of the 1920s had more choices. Jobs in social work, education, libraries, museums and the health industry (nursing and other caregiver jobs) offered them opportunities for upward mobility. They also had a louder voice in their relationships, which often spelled trouble in paradise. Interestingly enough, by 1928, the divorce rate had doubled. Not to say that "pink collar" workers were bringing home fat paychecks, as these women earned roughly half of what men earned. In fact, it would be about 50 more years before we would begin to see a significant bump in the number of women earning more money than their male partners.

Hard Times

As the roaring twenties came to a close, the largest financial disaster of the 20th century hit. The stock market crash of 1929 not only knocked Wall Street on its butt, it also primed the wheels of change both at home and at work. Jobs were hard to come by, unemployment soared and just putting food on the table was a challenge. I can remember my mom telling me stories that when she was a kid, sometimes all they had to eat for dinner was a can of green beans or some other non-perishable item. She also told me how my grandmother would walk both to and from work because she and my grandfather had gotten divorced, and she couldn't afford a car.

Despite sky-high unemployment, most men wouldn't stoop to taking jobs that were "deemed for women." As a result, many women found themselves becoming the main breadwinners of the household. Historically, this was the first time massive numbers of women faced the challenge of balancing work and home responsibilities. It also marked the first time that financial stress affected men and women of all ages, especially those men whose women were "bringing home the bacon" so to speak.

Economic hardships of the Depression made couples less likely to divorce, as individuals (especially women) stuck in unhappy marriages often decided to tough it out rather than risk financial ruin by leaving their spouses. Still, a small percentage of women began voicing their opinions both at work and at home. But their cries—at least initially—fell on deaf ears. After all, men still maintained a firm grasp on business and had a stronghold on key executive positions. Having earned the constitutional right to vote a decade earlier, women (especially working women) gradually became more vocal and grew more comfortable expressing their opinions. And these opinions no longer solely centered around home life, the kids and what was on the menu for dinner; they also included topics ranging from finances and politics to life planning. The winds of change were beginning to blow, as life started to become more about purpose then mere survival.

A Country At War

On the morning of December 7th, 1941, Japanese bombers unleashed a thunderstorm of bombs on Pearl Harbor. Not only did this vault the United States into World War II and permanently change the global landscape, it also ended the Depression and catapulted women (by the thousands) into the work force. While men went off to fight, women answered the call to support the war effort. During World War II, a whopping six million women entered the workforce for the first time, with hundreds of thousands taking on jobs previously dominated by men. Many worked in factories (as crane operators, in furniture production and in textile or garment manufacturing), and some even joined the armed forces—participating in every military field (nurses, pilots, clerks, communications staff) except combat. Their wages reached unprecedented levels, although the gender gap in pay persisted. Stepping up to keep the country operating was their "patriotic duty," as symbolized by *Life* Magazine's iconic "Rosie the Riveter." But despite long hours, women were expected to keep the home fires burning as well.

Once peace was declared, scores of women were laid off, since businesses and factories no longer needed so many workers. Besides, most positions that remained available were reserved for men returning from battle.

Many women were ecstatic to leave their temporary jobs and redirect their focus back to their homes and marriages. Others, not so much. Wartime work had given women newfound confidence in their abilities, not to mention the benefits of earning a paycheck when the cost of living was so high. As peacetime neared, the media did its best to convince married women to return home to look after their families. One example: *Ladies Home Journal* columnist Dorothy Thompson wrote, "...The ideal of every normal woman is to find the right husband, bear and rear his children and make with his earnings, for him and for them, a cozy, gay, happy home."

Statistics, however, did not back up that sentiment. After a brief lull, by 1947, the female labor force had resumed growing, and by 1948, for the first time in American history, married women outnumbered single women in the workforce. For men, this was clearly a wake-up call. More women working meant that men had to figure out how to manage women—and communicate with them—more effectively, both at work and at home.

Prosperity Reigns

The post-war era of the 1950s was all about growth. Families grew larger, the Gross National Product of the United States doubled, and as the country began shifting from an industrial to a service economy, employment opportunities for women exploded. But while the labor market beckoned women to "come aboard," many had conflicting emotions: frustration and boredom if they chose to stay at home; guilt if they opted to go to work.

As employers stepped up their efforts to lure moms into the labor force, psychologists and advice columnists insisted that marriage/motherhood was the most fulfilling career of all and warned women of the need to devote full-time attention to their husbands and children. Popular television shows of this decade underscored these messages. *Leave It To Beaver*, for instance, portrayed the iconic post-war American family: June, the perfect housewife; Ward, the hard-working dad; big brother Wally, and, of course the always mischievous little bro', Theodore (aka "The Beav"). In *The Donna Reed Show*, Donna was the perfect American housewife and mother—always neatly groomed, good-natured, thoughtful and capable. *Father Knows Best* depicted the classic wholesome family viewers could relate to and want to emulate. And *The Adventures of Ozzie and Harriet* featured the real-life Nelson family playing themselves. Their "adventures" involved very little conflict or friction, and problems or misunderstandings were always resolved quickly.

How to Be a Good Wife

The following is from a 1950s home economics textbook intended for high school girls, teaching them how to prepare for married life.

1. Have dinner ready. Plan ahead, even the night before, to have a delicious meal—on time. This is a way of letting him know that you have been thinking about him and are concerned about his needs. Most men are hungry when they come home, and the prospects of a good meal are part of the warm welcome needed.

2. Prepare yourself. Take 15 minutes to rest so you will be refreshed when he arrives. Touch up your makeup, put a ribbon in your hair and be fresh looking.

He has just been with a lot of work-weary people. Be a little gay and a little more interesting. His boring day may need a lift.

3. Clear away the clutter. Make one last trip through the main part of the house just before your husband arrives, gathering up schoolbooks, toys, paper, etc. Then run a dust cloth over the tables. Your husband will feel he has reached a haven of rest and order, and it will give you a lift, too.

4. Prepare the children. Take a few minutes to wash their hands and faces, comb their hair, and if necessary, change their clothes. They are little treasures, and he would like to see them playing the part.

5. Minimize the noise. At the time of his arrival, eliminate all noise of the washer, dryer, dishwasher or vacuum. Try to encourage the children to be quiet. Be happy to see him. Greet him with a warm smile.

6. Some Don'ts: Don't greet him with problems or complaints. Don't complain if he's late for dinner. Count this as minor compared with what he might have gone through that day.

7. Make him comfortable. Have him lean back in a comfortable chair or suggest he lie down in the bedroom. Have a cool or warm drink ready for him. Arrange his pillow and offer to take off his shoes. Speak in a low, soft, soothing and pleasant voice. Allow him to relax and unwind.

8. Listen to him. You may have a dozen things to tell him, but the moment of his arrival is not the time. Let him talk first.

9. Make the evening his. Never complain if he does not take you out to dinner or other places of entertainment. Instead, try to understand his world of strain and pressure, his need to be home and relax.

10. The goal: Try to make your home a place of peace and order where your husband can relax.

Yet, in the real world, post-war divorce rates continued to rise, as did fears over the state of marriage and family life. Gender roles were becoming blurred, and the coming decades would challenge the roles and responsibilities of both sexes, as well as begin to change the ways in which they communicated with each other.

You've Come A Long Way, Baby!

In the 1960s, the ranks of working women soared from 23 million to over 31 million. I could bore you with statistics all day long, but the takeaway here is that women were not only eager to enter the labor force, they wanted to climb the corporate ladder. Instead of staying home to watch the kids and the cave as their ancestors had done, women of this decade wanted to be the ones going out to gather the meat and bring it back at the end of the day.

Betty Friedan's landmark book, *The Feminine Mystique*, published in 1963, provides clues to women's growing discontent during this decade. In it, she describes the widespread unhappiness of women of the late '50s and early '60s who felt forced to be subservient to men financially, mentally, physically and intellectually. Friedan writes in the first pages of her book, that, at the end of the day, housewives were asking themselves, "Is that all?" *The Feminine Mystique* is widely credited with sparking the second wave of feminism in the United States. Case in point: the "bra-burning movement." Organized by women of the '50s who were tired of questioning their role in society and fed up with their less equal status relative to men, these women publicly set fire to their bras as a symbol to remove restrictions imposed upon them.

A slew of laws subsequently passed to help ambitious women reach their goals. The Equal Pay Act of 1963 and 1964 Civil Rights Act expanded women's claims to equal rights in the labor market. And Title IX of the Higher Education Act of 1972 empowered women to break gender barriers in undergraduate, graduate and professional training. By the end of the 1970s, growing numbers of women were becoming doctors, lawyers, dentists, scientists and engineers. "Me cave man, you cave woman" had become a distant memory.

But progress came with problems. If you're a fan of *Mad Men*, you can appreciate the critical acclaim it has received for its historical authenticity. Two characters in this series stand out as a sign of the times. Don Draper, a successful creative director and junior partner of an advertising agency, has a traditional marriage that ends in divorce due to his infidelities and because he and his wife (a homemaker) are total failures at communicating with one another. Peggy Olson rises from being Draper's secretary to being a copywriter with her own office, but she struggles to make her mark in this male-dominated field. Feeling increasingly underappreciated and patronized by Draper, Olson eventually leaves the firm to accept a better offer at a competing agency.

The challenges Don and Peggy face in *Mad Men* mirror those felt by many working men and women in the '60s and '70s. One glaring issue for women, for instance, was how to maintain their femininity while tapping into the "masculine dimensions" of their personalities to succeed in the "macho" business world. Not surprisingly women's "invasion" of the good 'ole boys' club left men feeling intimidated and mystified. Sure, they were accustomed to working women, but mainly in jobs "deemed" for women. Suddenly, they had to engage the fairer sex as colleagues, not subordinates, and that felt confusing, unfair, frustrating and improper to many.

Significant shifts were occurring on the home front as well. While sociological studies of families of the '60s and '70s reveal that husbands and wives were more likely than not to share decision making regarding child rearing, housing choices and family spending, women continued to perform the lion's share of household and child care duties. It's a no-brainer that this generated stress between husbands and wives, thus increasing the likelihood of a split. Little wonder that extramarital affairs began to increase. Ditto for divorce rates.

Staying Alive

As the Disco era began to fade, the music of Michael Jackson and Madonna ushered in the 1980s and eventually the 1990s. The landscape of marriages, home and work had undergone drastic changes—with more to come. With the cost of living on the rise, it was becoming increasingly difficult for families to survive on just one income. The feminist movement had taken hold, and many women were no longer content with traditional jobs. Instead, they had their eyes set on management and executive positions. By 1982, women outnumbered men receiving either bachelor or master's degrees, and women's employment was growing at twice the rate of men's. The wage gap between the sexes was narrowing, with some wage-earning wives making as much as their husbands, and women's ascent up the corporate ladder continued.

Gender discrimination lingered, however, barring women from most of the highest positions in government or industry, although women managed to snag executive level representation in virtually every occupation. "I am woman, hear me roar" was no longer just a sound, it carried a significant bite along with it. For men, times were changing and those winds of change I talked about earlier were accompanied by a Nordic wind chill.

Being a man had never been tougher. Relationship roles were becoming more difficult to define; family guidelines were a crossover from one to gender to the other. The term "Mr. Mom" was born, as men began to find themselves sharing the traditional roles women used to fill. Two working parents added stress to the family, and leisure time for both mom and dad was harder to come by. Couples attempted to adapt by altering or changing their work schedules to cover—or offset—the high costs of daycare. But, more often than not, this effort to keep their financial picture healthy only added to spouses spending less time together and certainly less quality time together.

In the early '90s, the previously academic-oriented Internet became more user-friendly for the average Joe, and record numbers of brick-and-mortar businesses began scrambling to gain a presence in cyberspace. Moreover, new online start-ups were starting to create a big buzz—Amazon, eBay, WebMD, Monster, etc. Investors poured trillions into these commercial Internet ventures, creating a dot-com boom—along with plenty of job opportunities for both men and women.

As the 21st Century approached, three out of five women worked, and over 50 percent of all married women were bringing home a paycheck. The bottom line: Traditional roles had fallen by the wayside, and home life was becoming more stressful. Since men were no longer the sole breadwinners, decision makers, providers and protectors of the family, many lacked direction and a sense of purpose. Women were no longer the stay-at-home wives, mothers, secretaries, cooks and housekeepers. Defined traditional roles had changed for both men and women—and not just at home, but at the office as well.

In the corporate world, women were making inroads in the boardroom. Executive seats were no longer "male-only" territory; women were finally figuring out how to play with the "big boys." Succeeding at that game, however, usually meant learning how to "swim" in the shark-like environment of the traditional business arena. Meanwhile, men were struggling to hold on to their "fraternity of corporate brotherhood," if you will. For most women, this environment felt foreign and called for them to develop a more "masculine" dimension to their business persona. This persona would suit them well at work, but it would be difficult to shed when they left the office and headed home. Again, with traditional roles being tossed out the window, couples were struggling to balance life at work with life at home. This cross-gender role-playing was creating an identity problem with both sexes, and that was making communication between the sexes more and more difficult.

A New Millennium

As a new century dawned, the artist formerly known as "Prince" encouraged us to "Party Like It's 1999." And how could we not? There was so much hype built up around Y2K that when the clock struck midnight on New Year's Eve, there were many who thought our technology grid was going to crash and that total chaos would ensue. The world woke up the next morning, and to the surprise of many, all was quiet on the Western Front. The economy was healthy, and the state of the union was good. The landscape of corporate and domestic America was continuing to change and evolve. On a daily basis, men and women faced the challenges of balancing their home lives with their professional lives. Record numbers of women had conquered the corporate boardroom, earning impressive salaries to match their impressive titles. Nevertheless, many women still struggled with fitting in and worked hard at not being perceived as "soft." Sometimes their efforts to be "tough enough" backfired. For instance, Anna Wintour, editor of *Vogue* magazine was nicknamed "The Ice Queen" and later became the muse for the film *The Devil Wears Prada*. And no one ever called Carly Fiorina, the head of Hewlett Packard from 1999 to 2005, a wilting lily. On the contrary, according to her memoir, *Tough Choices*, she was sometimes referred to as "Chainsaw Carly." Ouch!

By all accounts, these should have been celebratory times for women, but from the let's-be-careful-what-you-ask-for department, a sizeable portion of working women were discovering that while their career or corporate success felt great, they weren't able to enjoy their accomplishments as much as they would like. The question had to be asked: "Were women becoming the new men?" What price were they paying by bouncing back and forth between their jobs and home? Studies show that women at every level were still leaving the office and working a "second shift" at home—caring for husbands and children (if they had them), doing most of the housework and looking after elder relatives. So, the downsides to women's new workforce power were: stress, pressure, exhaustion, burn-out and heart attacks—which was exactly what used to kill hard-driving corporate men—and sometimes still does. Much like walking into a pitch dark room with no lights, women began feeling a bit lost and off balance with the overall scope of their lives.

For men, adapting to the new XY (men and women) family dynamic was proving to be equally challenging. Nothing is more sensitive at times than the male ego, and clearly that ego was being pushed, pulled, twisted and often hung out to dry. I speak from experience when I say that having your female spouse make more money than you do can be a bit of a blow, since historically, men are used to being the breadwinners and providers of the family. Like a boxer who has sustained a powerful right hook, thousands of men found themselves feeling dazed and a bit confused when it came to managing their lives.

As if things weren't bad enough, the early- and mid-2000s brought three major global developments that would put even more strain on both professional and domestic relationships. First up was the dot-com bust, which started in early 2000 when the bottom began to fall out of the dot-com industry. By 2004, more than half of the Internet companies created since 1995 were gone, and hundreds of thousands of tech workers were out of jobs.

Next up was September 11, 2001, a day that no American will ever forget. This was a day that would thrust our country back into war and a day that would have ripple effects for years to come with military families coast to coast (and with *all* American families in terms of feeling safe and secure). Relationships are hard enough, but add sending your husband or wife off to war to the mix, and it's certainly not the best-case scenario for having the perfect relationship or marriage.

Finally, in 2007-08, the greatest economic downturn since the Depression of the 1930s hit. Every family was affected in some way. The bottom literally fell out of the housing market. Home values stagnated at first, then began declining. Homeowners from coast to coast struggled to make their mortgage payments. Foreclosures occurred in the thousands, then soared into the tens of thousands. The stock market reacted, and more importantly, corporate America reacted by tightening their belts, cutting expenses, slashing jobs and slicing salaries. The unemployment rate began to rise, the job market grew increasingly competitive and jobs became more and more scarce.

The economic downturn hit men the hardest. They held nearly 80 percent of jobs—from Silicon Valley to Blue Collar America—that were lost during what is now being called the "mancession." Millions of Americans—both men and women—found themselves either out of work or forced to take jobs making less money. Needless to say, the economic strain these events put on relationships was intense. Couples were no longer just dealing with gender roles and communication issues, they were trying to figure out how to keep their families fed and housed.

Here and Now

With the economy starting to stabilize (albeit, slower than we'd like) and the wheels of corporate America beginning to churn at full strength again, the same old communication problems dual-income couples typically encounter have returned. These run the gamut from money and sex, to how to raise kids, and how to carve out quality time to spend together. Long ago, men and women had clearly defined roles and responsibilities, enabling them to live/work in harmony. Today those roles—at work and at home—have blurred. Women make up nearly 50 percent of the American workforce and in almost two-fifths of American families, women are the primary or co-breadwinners. What's more, in cases where both husbands and wives work, about one-fifth of the women earn more than their spouses.

But enough about statistics and history. Let's move on to present day and cracking the gender code. Men may be from Mars, and women may be from Venus, but to thrive and prosper on Planet Earth now, you need to understand what makes the opposite sex tick today. Only then will you have the tools you truly need to revolutionize your relationships—both at work and at home.

Chapter Two

THE X AND Y FACTOR

Mirror, Mirror on the wall, why do men
drive me the craziest of all?

Mirror, Mirror on the wall why do
women drive me straight up the wall?

Since the dawn of time, men and women have been trying to figure each other out. In the structure of modern-day relationships, both sexes are challenged—daily—to work and live in harmony with the opposite sex. Oftentimes, this is way easier said than done. What's become crystal clear is that men and women think, act and react emotionally, intellectually, professionally and domestically in unique ways. Not to say that either sex is better than the other...sorry guys! Men and women are just different, with each sex possessing his or her own strengths.

The One-Two Punch of Nature and Nurture

To get a grasp on what makes each sex "tick," we must travel back to the beginning of life. Other than the obvious chromosomal and anatomical differences, research reveals that males and females are exposed to different hormones in vitro, and scientists believe those hormones can actually influence behavior and attitude outside a mother's womb.

Once out in the real world, there's even more scientific evidence that little boys and little girls are raised differently. Even parents attempting to raise "gender neutral" kids fail for the most part. In other words, when raising their children, the majority of moms and dads tend to revert back to what "feels right." In fact, studies show that maternal and paternal instincts are potent, powerful and almost impossible to suppress.

One fascinating study I found talks about how, from birth, parents begin (usually subconsciously) to send gender specific messages to their kids. Fathers, for instance, will often choose words like *soft, delicate, cute* and *beautiful* to describe their little girls. When it comes to describing their little boys, however, they'll typically use words like, *strong, alert, well coordinated* and *firm*. This research hit home with me, as I can remember doing this very same thing with my daughter.

In another telling experiment, researchers observed five mothers taking turns playing individually with "Adam," a six-month-old infant who was dressed in blue. Later, six different mothers were observed playing with "Beth," the same infant, then dressed in pink. Isolated in a room and given three toys (a plastic fish, a doll and a train) for entertaining the infants, most mothers chose the train to entertain "Adam" and the doll to entertain "Beth." The mothers also interacted differently with the infants, depending on whether they thought they were playing with a girl or a boy. "Beth," for example, received more smiles and hugs than "Adam" did. Yet, in post-observation interviews, *all eleven mothers* said they believed infants should be treated in the same way!

As children make the jump from infancy to pre-school and elementary school, these patterns continue. As youngsters begin to seek their independence, parents, especially mothers, encourage young boys to get outside, run free and play, but they have a tendency to shadow little girls. Having a younger sister, I can remember that's exactly what my mom did with us. The Reed boys had a separate set of rules, which allowed us to take more risks, be more adventurous and push the envelope further. My sister, however, grew up with a more sheltered set of guidelines.

When little boys get out of line, their behavior is often written off as, "Oh well, boys will be boys." Mischievous girls are not typically so fortunate. I can remember when I was about five or six, my immediate older brother got a hold of my sister's favorite stuffed animal (a bunny rabbit) and, acting like a "boy," he tied a noose around its neck and began running around the house. My sister was just steps behind him yelling, "Stop hanging my bunny...stop!" While she was almost in tears, my mom, who was laughing hysterically at the thought of a stuffed animal being hung, ordered my brother to take the noose off the bunny and give it back. But Mom didn't scold or punish my brother. To her, this was just an example of boys being boys, I guess. Conversely, if my sister acted out in a similar fashion, we would usually run to my mom, tell on our sister immediately, and my mom would reprimand her with a, "Young ladies don't act that way."

The Sandbox and Beyond

Have you ever sat and watched kids interact on a playground? Better yet, think back to the days when you spent time there yourself. Playground scenes offer great insight into how femininity and masculinity are established. In fact, observing the ways boys and girls at play communicate is much like watching the "coming attractions" at a movie theater, in that their clashing styles almost set the stage for how men and women tend to communicate as adults.

Think about it. On the playground, boys tend to play in large groups that are structured hierarchically (baseball, soccer, kick ball). Their groups typically have a leader, and their games almost always have winners and losers. Girls, however, tend to play in small groups or in pairs, where intimacy is the key. In their popular games (house, Barbie, jump rope, hopscotch), everyone gets a turn, and there are no winners or losers. Generally speaking boys at play are more competitive than girls are. They like to brag about their skills and argue about whose best at what. Their mantra: "If I beat you, I'm better than you." Girls, on the other hand, tend to be less competitive but more catty. They generally challenge each other and vie for status by comparing clothes, hairstyles, etc. Sometimes when sitting together and talking, a "wolf mentality" surfaces as they badmouth others who are "different" from them (typically behind others' backs) to make themselves feel superior.

Little boys play rough, and when one gets hurt the others will usually drag him off the field and continue to play. For them, the game is more important than the individual players. On the flip side, little girls will usually stop a game when someone gets hurt and wait until the injured player recovers. For them, the individual players take priority over the game. Boys at play issue commands without giving reasons for them. Example: "I'm captain today...Rick is on my team; you can have Frank." And when someone disputes the rules in a boys' game, the others are likely to say something like, "Either you play by the rules or get out of the game."

Girls, on the other hand, typically make proposals by saying, "Let's ..." or "Hey, what if we?" followed by reasons for their suggestions. It's their way of avoiding confrontation. And when someone suggests a better idea about a rule in a girls' game, there's a tendency for everyone to discuss the idea, change some of the rules and try a new version of the game.

Finally, boys fight frequently when they play--about twenty times as often as girls do, studies show. But they are also able to resolve their differences quickly and effectively. In fact, research reveals that boys who argue with each other often end up being *better* friends after the fight. Girls don't argue as often—at least not openly—but when they do, the bad feelings last—often for weeks. In fact, their arguments not only tend to end girls' games, but also can lead to realignments within social groups.

Can you see some of the foreshadowing I talked about earlier...how several of these characteristics and behaviors present on the playground translate into adult behavior at work and at home? There's no question that the socialization of boys and girls as they grow up has a huge impact, creating the foundation of so many traits they'll carry into adulthood. However, to think that all the X and Y differences men and women have can be traced from the womb, to parenting and back to the playground would leave us with an incomplete picture. Like a detective trying to solve a crime, there's a key piece of information still remaining that must be discussed: our brains.

Gray Matters

As discussed in Chapter One, as men and women evolved, their brains adapted to help them function, perform and master their specific roles. Women evolved as child bearers and nest defenders and, as a result, female brains became hardwired to nurture, nourish, love and care for the people in their lives. Men evolved with a completely different job description. They were hunters, chasers, protectors, providers and problem solvers. Scientific research, especially new high tech brain scans, confirms all of this.

Résumé

JANE DOE'S BRAIN

"Employment History"
The Gatherer. Responsibilities included collecting food near the cave and caring for children.

Primary Areas of Expertise
Speech and language, an area determined to be 30% larger (than in male brains). Also boasts 11% more brain cells in the temporal lobe, a region associated with language. Excels at tests measuring word recall and other tests of verbal memory. Superior at remembering landmarks and where objects are located.

Strengths
• Ability to multitask. Especially proficient at using both sides of the brain simultaneously and performing several different tasks at once, due to enhanced development of the corpus callosum (connecting tissue between the right and left hemispheres).

• Intuitive. Thanks to supersensory abilities, can quickly detect a wide range of emotions, both verbal and nonverbal, and better understand what's going on below the surface.

• People person. Hard wired to respond to faces and emotions. Also boasts higher levels of oxytocin, a brain chemical associated with feeling connected to others.

• Team player. Communicates to get closer to and involve others. Prefers to make decisions by gathering data, weighing variables and considering multiple options, outcomes and points of view.

Weaknesses
• Sensitive. Tendency to take criticism personally. Also holds grudges, as internal hard drive tends to store every emotional slight.

• Transparent. Easy access to both brain hemispheres make it sometimes difficult to hide feelings and emotions.

Résumé

JOHN DOE'S BRAIN

"Employment History"
The Hunter. Responsibilities included killing large animals for food and clothing, defending the homestead and protecting loved ones from enemies.

Primary Areas of Expertise
Spatial skills, such as mechanical design, measurements, directions, and manipulation of physical objects. Excels at tests measuring high-end mathematical reasoning. Also superior at navigating along a specific route.

Strengths

• Focused. A smaller hippocampus in the limbic system and less corpus callosum (connecting tissue between the two sides of the brain) doesn't allow emotions to get in the way when making important decisions.

• Risk taker. Driven to succeed. Higher levels of testosterone fuel a need for challenge and competition.

• Resourceful. Logical, problem-solving mind is programmed to offer solutions (even when not solicited).

• Take-charge attitude. Communicates primarily to get need-to-know information across to others and to gain control. Also, higher levels of the brain chemical vasopressin lead to feelings of territoriality and a preference for operating within a hierarchy.

Weaknesses

• Impatient/impulsive. Tendency to act or speak before thinking, due to lower serotonin levels (the brain's "brakes") and a higher volume of spinal fluid (which moves physical impulses from the brain to the body).

• Tunnel vision. Can only focus on one thing at a time, due to 30% fewer (and more compartmentalized) connecting fibers between the right and left hemispheres.

Reprinted with permission from *GenderTalk Works,* by Connie Glaser

He Says, She Says

The primary reason men and women struggle with communication is because they simply don't understand each other. Let's take a look at some of the more common and most problematic differences that tend to create the great gender divide...

- **He's blunt; she hedges.** When it comes to communication, men tend to be straight shooters. Their sentences are typically short, direct and "tell it like it is." Example: "My team is going to make budget this month." This type of speech is usually associated with confidence and competence. Interestingly enough, men will often speak with certainty even when they're *not* sure they're right (maybe his team doesn't have a chance in hell of making budget!). Women, on the other hand, tend to soften—even "sugarcoat"—their statements. You'll often hear them hedge, utter disclaimers or use tag questions. Examples: "I'm pretty sure my team will make budget this month," "I *think* my team will make budget this month," or "We're definitely going make budget this month, right?" Women use these styles of speech even when they *are* 100% sure, and they tend to do it because they're always considering others' feelings. But men don't see what feelings have to do with it.

The masculine style of influencing behavior also uses commanding language. A man might tell his team, or staff, "Here is what we need to get done today." Meanwhile, the feminine approach is typically more persuasive in nature. A woman is more likely to say, "I have an idea that I want run by you." Or she may phrase her idea as a question: "Let me ask you, 'What do you think of this idea?'" Traditionally speaking, the masculine style is more closely linked to leadership and power, while the feminine style is viewed as a less commanding approach. And let's not forget to factor in tone of voice. Leadership and authority are typically associated with a deep, "masculine" tone, not a softer, higher pitched "feminine" tone. This doesn't mean that women need to drop their voices an octave to be perceived as authoritative; it simply means that women are more challenged to monitor their tone of voice and be direct when delivering a message.

Even as kids, boys tend to be blunt!

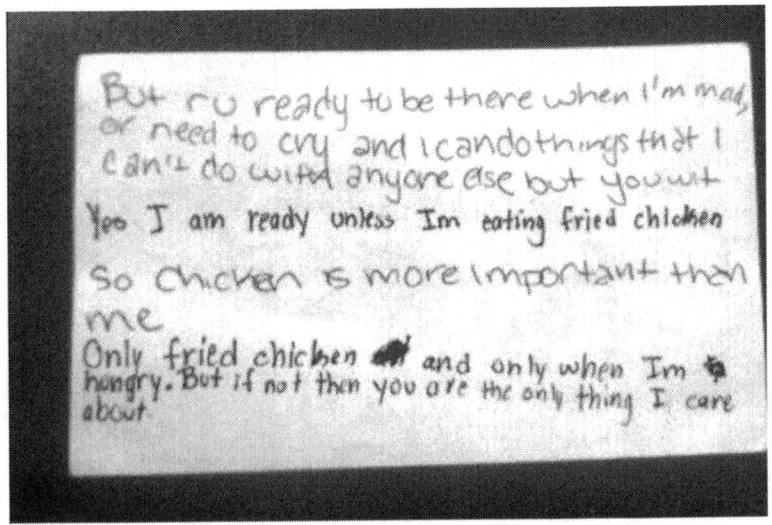

Anytime I think or write about speaking with an authoritative tone, I immediately hear my dad's voice in my head. My older brother, Tim, and I both played varsity basketball for our high school, and my dad never missed a game. What was so funny is that by the time I stepped into the spotlight, I noticed that my mom wouldn't sit with my dad during the games. You see, my dad never met a referee that he really liked and would voice his opinion often when he didn't agree with a ref's call. The problem was, in a gym full of students and parents, you could hear him loud and clear. Our family almost wore his booming voice as a badge of honor. If you supported the Springbrook Blue Devils, you knew Ray Reed was there to support you. And if you ever have the opportunity to hear me speak in person, you'll know that my dad passed a little bit of that voice on to his son.

• **Decisions, decisions.** When it comes to making decisions, men "hunt" and women "gather." We established these characteristics in Chapter One, and here's how they surface in the decision-making process. As "gatherers," women tend to explore multiple possibilities, weigh a number of variables and consider various outcomes or options. Men, on the other hand, are "hunters" and focused simply on finding answers—usually as quickly as possible. Men don't like to ponder when it comes to making decisions; their desire is to complete the task at hand. Like oil and water, these decision-making processes can create gender conflict. For example, men often think women are trying to manipulate or undermine a business meeting if they introduce what men may perceive as a mound of unnecessary data. Even worse, since women don't think in a linear, step-by-step fashion as men often do, some men regard women as less rational, less logical, less precise and, dare I say, less intelligent. It's my opinion that this perception is changing, but not fast enough.

Three years ago, I worked with Stacy, who held a middle management position at a Fortune 500 company and was eager to make the leap to upper management. Stacy was bright, articulate, adored by her team and a star player at contributing to her company's bottom line. But when a higher-level position became available, she wasn't even granted an interview. When Stacy came to me, she was frustrated and ready to jump ship. I encouraged her to ask her immediate boss for his opinion on why she was overlooked for the higher position. What she learned surprised her. On the positive side, Stacy was lauded for her positive attitude, strong leadership skills and for always meeting—and usually exceeding—her team's goals. On the downside, however, she was criticized for "drowning" upper management with excessive details and information—in proposals, summaries, presentations and emails. Once Stacy learned to write and speak more concisely, using bullet points and less verbiage, she was promoted.

• **Read my hips.** Science tells us that the communication center inside a woman's brain is larger than the one inside a man's brain. For this reason, women are generally better at processing words and understanding what others are really saying. I'm sure any woman reading this is probably saying, "Duh, known that for a long time." Women also excel at reading between the lines and are far more tuned into reading body language and facial expressions than men are. For any guy out there that's ever heard the phrase, "What does *that* look mean?" you know what I'm talking about.

• **I've got a problem.** Consider the classic scenario where a couple is traveling somewhere together by car, and they get lost. I'm sure you've been there, done that. More than likely, if you're a woman, you suggested pulling into a gas station to ask for directions. But if you're a man, that's usually not an option. Most men would rather stay lost for another hour and eventually find the location on their own. To them, asking for directions is a sign of "defeat," or an admission that they can't solve their own problems.

When it comes to problem solving, there are gender discrepancies in the ways men and women express themselves as well. Women tend to solve problems by thinking out loud. Ladies, if you tend to call on friends or relatives to discuss various options and possibilities to whatever dilemma you're facing, you know what I mean. There's also a lot of emotion involved when women problem solve. Scientists tell us that's because a woman's brain literally has billions of neuroconnections between her talk center and the area of her brain that processes feelings. The result is literally a "superhighway" connecting what she feels with what she says.

Men will talk about a problem, too, but they tend to do so silently to themselves. In fact, brain scans reveal that in the midst of solving a problem, men actually have conversations with themselves. Scientists suspect that men are more likely to ponder in silence because their brains are organized to problem-solve first and experience emotions second. This probably also allows men to feel more in control.

And remember those "superhighways" women's brains have? Male brains don't have them. In fact, if you could look inside the average male mind, you'd more likely find a flashing sign that says, "Road under Construction!" That's because when a man experiences an emotion, he first decides if he wants to address it and speak about it, then he moves over to the left side of his brain so he can begin formulating his thoughts into words. And as he begins expressing himself and new emotions begin to surface, he literally has to begin this process all over again.

This is one reason why men and women struggle so much during an emotional conversation. For women, it's natural to communicate emotions and thoughts together, but for men it's like asking us to rub our heads in a circular motion while simultaneously patting our bellies (how many of us tried to pull that off when we were kids?).

• **Got stress?** Stressful situations are often accompanied by a "fight or flight" response in men. In fact, studies show that when men feel tense, testosterone orders neuroreceptors in their brains to drop everything and react as quickly as possible. This explains why, when men are stressed, they either dig in their heels and prepare for an altercation, or they simply exit stage left and fall off the grid for a few hours. In fact, studies show that when men get angry or frustrated it takes about 30 minutes for the chemicals in their body to get back to center. In other words, there is no "arguing" with an angry male. He needs time—and space.

On the flip side, when women feel frazzled, their reaction is to "tend and befriend." Translated, that means women skirt physical responses and look for someone to talk to about their feelings. Remember, her brain is prewired to use speech as a main form of expression, so talking things out is the best way she knows to release pent-up frustrations.

• **The energizer bunny vs. the space cadet.** Studies show that the female mind is constantly working overtime. I can speak to this directly, as I have a close female friend whose brain, I swear, never shuts down. I often tease her during conversation when she bounces from one topic to another at the drop of a hat. She can effortlessly discuss a myriad of topics and process multiple thoughts, while I sometimes struggle to process just one. To any female reading this book, I don't have to tell you that the male brain will occasionally "space out." Stop laughing, ladies...lol. Indeed, research reveals that when a man's brain is in its resting state, approximately 70 percent of its electrical activity is shut down. But during that same state, a woman's brain shows approximately 90 percent activity.

• **Getting from here to there.** Ask a man for directions to his house, and you're going to get very detailed information about how to get there: "Take the Frontage Road for 3.3 miles. At the four-way stop, hang a left on to Eastbourne Drive, go one block and our driveway is the second one on the right. Ask a women the same question, however, and she's likely to get you there using landmarks: "Pass the mall, turn left at the Exxon station, then turn right at the elementary school. Go a few blocks more and look for the house with the huge flower garden on the left."

Researchers say these gender differences line up with different brain regions. Neuroscientists have found that women use the central cortex (an area that transforms emotions into thoughts) when they navigate, while men use a part of the brain that's devoted to memory storage, a quality that is not activated in a woman's brain during navigational tasks. For similar reasons, men tend to best women when it comes to reading maps. Turns out, this is a "talent" related to spatial abilities, which brain scans show are located in the right front brain for men and is one of a male's strongest abilities.

To understand this, let's revisit the Stone Age for a minute. Remember that men evolved as hunters and would have to calculate speed, movement and distance of prey, then determine how much force would be needed to kill their lunch or dinner with a rock or spear before calculating how to get back home. In women, on the other hand, spatial ability is located in both brain hemispheres, but it doesn't have a specific measurable location like it does in men. In fact, only about 10 percent of women have spatial abilities that are comparable to most men.

• **You call that funny?** What makes men and women laugh can be very different. MRI scans show that a man's "funny bone" is located on the right frontal lobe, just above the eye. But for women, additional areas of the brain—like the left prefrontal cortex—are engaged when processing humor, which researchers believe suggests a greater emphasis on language and executive processing. Scientists say this could very well explain why most men enjoy visual humor (like slapstick comedy), while women prefer humor with a bit more depth.

• **"Laws" of attraction.** How do the sexes differ when it comes to attraction and sex? I doubt it will shock either sex to learn that the area inside the brain responsible for "sexual desire" is larger in a man's brain, and as result:

✓ Men think about sex more often than women do.

✓ Men put more emphasis on looks than women do.

✓ Men become attached to a woman just because she looks hot.

✓ Men are stimulated visually, causing them to often get in trouble with their significant other when out in public and they notice another attractive female. A man won't get in trouble for looking at a really cool sports car that just drove by, but gaze upon another woman and watch out!

✓ Women do care about a man's physical appearance, but they tend to put more emphasis on personality, intelligence and feeling a connection.

✓ Women generally seek an emotional connection before becoming sexual.

✓ Women tend to be more romantic than men.

Can you identify with any of the gender differences discussed in this chapter? Do you recognize traits or behaviors that are present in you, your partner, your boss or coworkers? Gaining knowledge about the opposite sex and educating yourself more about your own gender "quirks" are extremely powerful tools. Building a successful relationship—either at home or at work—calls for attention to detail and awareness of both your behavior and the behavior of those with whom you interact. I challenge myself daily to never stop learning and to pay attention to my own behavior and, as you read this book, I encourage you to do the same.

In this chapter, we've unlocked a handful of biological mysteries and explored cultural issues that cause men and women to be motivated by different things and have different needs. I hope that this knowledge, along with the tips and tools I'll share in the next five chapters, will go a long way in helping you avoid misunderstandings that gender differences create in the workplace and on the home front. At the end of the day, there's no question that men and women *are* different. Neither is better or worse; we're just different. Sure, these disparities cause a lot of conflict and turmoil, but they are also a huge part of what makes life interesting.

Remember, cracking the gender code isn't about keeping score. It's all about finding ways for both sexes to understand and respect where the other is "coming from." And I firmly believe that when we all focus on appreciating—even celebrating—our differences, that's when both men *and* women thrive.

Chapter Three

THE DUMBO EFFECT

Have you ever heard the old cliché, "I'm all ears?" In the case of the famous Walt Disney elephant, Dumbo, that was exactly the case. Dumbo's big ears eventually served him well, and for anyone looking to become a more effective communicator, using your ears to work on being a better listener is critical.

Most of us *claim* to be great listeners, yet studies show that the majority of people only listen for approximately 25 percent of the time. Moreover, in many cases, most people only listen to the first couple of words before starting to formulate a response in their minds. This chapter will emphasize the paramount importance of listening and the magical effects of being "all ears." It will also elaborate on how having the "memory of an elephant" can strengthen your professional and personal relationships.

The reality for most people is, you probably don't listen as effectively as you think you do, and chances are, you're not even aware of it. Think about it for a minute. When's the last time you took a personal inventory of your strengths and weaknesses, looked yourself in the mirror and exclaimed, "Yep, I really suck at listening...I mean *really* suck." I'm guessing never, but a recent study of over 8,000 people employed in business, the military, hospitals, universities and government agencies found that *virtually all of the participants* believed that they communicated effectively—or more effectively than their friends, families and coworkers. Again, research reveals that the average person listens at only about 25 percent efficiency. Wait a second!!! That's huge! Could it be that everyone is above average? I don't think so.

Take a minute to imagine your normal day and all the people you come in contact with. Then imagine that you may be hearing what all of those people are telling you with only a 25 percent efficiency rate. WOW! That means you're potentially missing out on a whopping 75 percent of what's being said to you. Even more concerning is that while most people agree that listening effectively is a very important skill, most people don't feel a strong need to improve their own skill levels. After reading this chapter, I'm hopeful that you'll take inventory of how well you listen and take steps to boost your skills.

What's in it for you? Plenty! Becoming a better listener gives you the power to:

✓ Reduce misunderstandings, as well as nasty and/or unnecessary arguments.

✓ Dazzle others by making them feel special, understood and connected to you.

✓ Unearth "gold nuggets" of information that you can use to your advantage.

✓ Develop and nurture new and existing friendships.

✓ Improve your marriage and love life.

✓ Boost your professional profits, as well as your personal bottom line.

✓ Help advance your career.

✓ Turn you into a "people magnet," since people love to spend time with those that listen well and make them feel good.

✓ Allow you to gather and collect more information from the people you interact with daily.

✓ Increase others' trust in you.

✓ Reduce the amount of conflict you have in your life both at home and work.

✓ Help you to understand what motivates people.

✓ Inspire a higher level of commitment from the people you manage.

✓ Remember things about a person and what's going on in their lives, which results in a more effective connection.

Since we've already established that most people aren't great listeners, does that mean we're lazy, uncommitted or just careless? The answer is NO!!! Truth be told, listening is NOT a simple skill. In fact, becoming a good listener is fairly complex, but we know that the success of our marriages, friendships, and work relationships depends heavily upon mastering this skill. So much of the advice offered by "experts" focuses on the technical aspect of listening—like giving feedback, making good eye contact (which is important), asking open-ended questions and not interrupting others when they're speaking. All of these factors definitely play a role in listening, but they don't get to the core and empower you to become a better listener. Here are some key points to consider:

- **Listening should be active, not passive.** You may assume that "active" listening merely means making eye contact and uttering affirmative sounds ("uh huh," "I see") or nodding your head now and then to show you're hearing what's being said. Well, think again. Active listening actually involves not just *hearing* the words that are being spoken, but also *absorbing* what's being said. To do this, you need to allow yourself to get a sense of who the person is, how they view life, what they're hoping to accomplish by talking to you, the concerns they have, what their fears are, how they are feeling at that moment and what they may or not want from you.

Active listening also entails "listening" to what people *aren't* saying—at least directly—as well as what they may be to reluctant to say, or what they don't want you to do in response to their communication. So, in order to become a master communicator and listener, you can't be satisfied with just hearing the words people speak. You must factor in the many other dimensions that result in the total message being delivered.

When you consider all these factors that go into being an active listener, it's no wonder why it's so difficult to recognize what good listeners do that make them so successful. In essence, they are like sponges. During a conversation they're absorbing everything they can—both mentally and physically.

- **Listening for unspoken messages.** These could be concerns, dreams, unspoken fears and signs or signals indicating what kind of mood the person you're listening to is in. Whenever anybody speaks, they always reveal their most inner thoughts, ambitions and concerns. The trouble is, few listeners actually pick up on these subtle cues. Good listeners, however, pay attention and factor in these unspoken emotions and concerns. And when they hear them and empathize—verbally or nonverbally—the speaker often acknowledges (usually silently), "Man, you really understand me!" or "Wow, you really do get how I'm feeling."

• **Listening with respect and validation.** Want in on a big secret regarding how to become a better listener? Take on the task of finding something to respect and/or validate about what your conversation partner is saying. Then prove it by uttering statements like, "I hear what you're saying," or "That's a very valid point you make." This may sound shockingly simple, yet only one out of 100 people realizes how important a step this is in the listening process. The thing is, people often spend time listening for faults or weaknesses in what the other person is saying. Moreover, it's not uncommon that people disagree—either verbally or silently—with the other person's opinions, attitudes or point of view.

Of course, nobody likes to have other people disagree with his/her point of view, but we all know that this is going to happen from time to time. Nevertheless, we at least want our thoughts and feelings to be respected and equally considered—even if/when our opinions or attitudes are off the mark or based on bad information. The bottom line here is that if you can't make people feel that you respect their point of view, they won't feel "understood" and will label you as a "bad listener."

That's what happened to Scott, an insurance sales executive. When his company transferred him from Buffalo to Phoenix, he had trouble connecting with his new sales staff, many of whom left the company within a year after his arrival. This sudden high turnover led Human Resources to have all employees evaluate their supervisors. Scott earned dismal ratings for his listening skills. Comments from his disgruntled team included: "He makes decisions based on past experiences at his former office and is not open to our input," "He almost always interrupts us when we try to express our concerns," and "On rare occasions when he solicits our advice, he quickly discounts our ideas—sometimes even making fun of them."

- **Making listening a one way street.** One of the most important tips I give my clients when it comes to listening is to stop thinking about how you're going to respond to what a person is saying prior to them finishing speaking. It's difficult, if not impossible, to become a good listener if you're not first taking in the *entire* message being communicated to you. Unfortunately, the majority of the time when we're listening, our minds are hard at work formulating a response to a thought that hasn't been fully presented. The only way to truly absorb a message is to remain 100 percent focused on the person speaking and the words coming out of his/her mouth. This involves taking in the words they're speaking, the emotions they're feeling and actively working to put yourself in their shoes.

A good way to master this technique is to pause for three to four seconds after they stop speaking to really digest what is being said. Nothing is more flattering than knowing that someone else is really listening to every word you are saying. Another trick that works: Try rewording what they have said occasionally and repeat it back to them. This is a great way to make them others valued and important.

Above all, focus on keeping your mind clear, open and ready to discover the value of that person's message. This process requires focus and conscious effort, and it cannot be accomplished if you're battling your own thoughts instead of absorbing theirs. You may not always be successful at this, but the more conscious you are about it, the greater your chances are for success.

• **Listening for trouble on the horizon.** Another secret on the path to becoming a great listener is training yourself to listen for potential trouble or disaster. Most people don't just come right out and tell you that they're upset, angry or irritated with you. They often don't have the confidence to handle confrontation or would prefer to avoid conflict (this, as well as tips on resolving conflict will be covered in an upcoming chapter), but they will offer signs and clues that they are not happy campers. Some will even convince themselves that they *are* communicating these feelings to you directly, and when you fail to pick up on their subtle clues, they will see this as further proof that you aren't interested or that you don't really care about their feelings.

This commonly occurs in both business and personal relationships. At work, a team leader promises to complete a project by a certain date, but when asked how it's going, he's not revealing details that would indicate a lot of progress has been made. At home, our significant other may drop subtle hints to let us know that we've done something wrong, or he/she may become agitated with some aspect of our behavior. They might not come right out and say what's bugging them directly, but they will expect you to detect the problem and take action to fix it.

In my experience women, more so than men, want their partner to do a better job of reading their moods and interpreting their thoughts. Good thing the next chapter is about non-verbal communication! The reality is, the more you train yourself to "listen" for these little signs of trouble, the better you will appreciate what's going on with those with whom you communicate most often. Listening for people's level of commitment, integrity and character is an incredibly useful skill. Listening for sincerity is equally advantageous. These skills are not difficult to develop, but mastering them does require practice and effort. I challenge you to increase your level of awareness and begin noticing and listening out for the little things you probably passed over before.

- **Listening without interrupting.** If you interrupt folks when they're talking, it not only prevents them from finishing or completing their thought, it also sends a message that you're not really interested in the rest of what they have to say—and that what you have to say is more important. Constant interruptions can also create havoc in both professional and personal relationships.

I recently received an email from Sean and Abby, who had dated in college, lived together for a year and then got married. Soon after celebrating their first wedding anniversary, they began experiencing some major problems communicating. The frustration of not being heard and understood soon escalated into major disagreements and nasty, heated arguments. Both complained that the other was guilty of constant interruptions. In an effort to improve this couple's listening skills, I encouraged Sean and Abby to grab an object whenever they were having a discussion, and the rule was, whoever was holding that object "had the floor"—meaning that the other person was obligated to listen and could not speak until the object was passed to them. A big part of what makes Sean and Abby's story so endearing is that the object this couple chose to use during potentially heated discussions was a stuffed penguin Sean had won for Abby at the state fair when they were dating. During a discussion, whoever had the penguin in their possession had the floor, and the other person had to wait for the penguin to be passed to them before speaking or responding. Almost immediately, Sean and Abby began to experience and absorb what was being said to them. They not only heard the words, they also started paying closer attention to each other's tone of voice, facial expressions and the emotions behind the message being delivered. In a very short time, their relationship started to heal, and Sean and Abby began to reconnect.

Sean and Abby made a wise choice in choosing a stuffed penguin for their object. For starters, it had sentimental value to both of them, which helped to remind them of their love for one another. Second, both agreed that because the object they chose was playful and a bit silly, their disagreements seemed to end more quickly. That makes total sense...can you imagine having a heated argument with your partner when they're clutching a stuffed animal?

The Listening Gap

There's one more challenge to becoming a more effective listener, and this is a big one. Since a slew of research tells us that men and women listen differently, obviously, understanding these disparities is also key to honing your listening skills. What are the most glaring gender differences in this area that you need to know about? Listen up...

• **Men listen with half a brain.** Literally! Brain scans reveal that men rely mostly on the left side of their brain while listening, while women use both sides. This explains how women can have a face-to-face conversation with one person, while monitoring another conversation nearby. It also explains why men sometimes struggle to focus on a conversation when there's significant background noise—like a blaring TV or other people nearby having a loud conversation. Lesson learned here: Removing all distractions is usually key to making sure a man hears and understands what you're saying.

• **Men listen like statues.** Women often accuse men of not listening when they really are—they just don't *look* like they are. It's their lack of expression or emotion that makes males appear to be tuning out the person who's talking to them. But studies show men wear this "mask" merely to show they're in control and to avoid revealing any emotions that may make them appear weak. Remember, guys evolved as warriors, protectors and problem solvers, so they are conditioned not to show fear or uncertainty.

Another gender clash that leads women to believe that men aren't listening occurs when she asks his opinion or thoughts about how to solve a problem, then waits for his reply. And waits...and waits, finally assuming he didn't hear a word she said. Usually, that's not the case at all. While women tend to think out loud, men are more likely to talk silently to themselves. In other words, if you ask a man to solve a problem, he'll often respond, "I got this; leave it to me," or "Let me think it over." And that's exactly what men do—they begin to think it over silently.

Deep in thought, most men will show little expression until the combination to the safe has been figured out, and they finally crack the code to the problem or dilemma. Only then—and usually with great enthusiasm—will they reveal the solution. In fact, this is how in today's world a man can still show you he's the hunter—or your hero. So remember ladies, silence on a man's part doesn't mean he's ignoring you or not interested in what you have to say. More often than not, he's formulating a thought or just having his own little internal conversation.

We Interrupt This Chapter To Discuss...INTERRUPTIONS!

In studies comparing conversations between men and women with those just between men, interruptions in all the conversations between men only were balanced. However, when a man and women were speaking, the man interrupted the woman 96 percent more often than the woman interrupted the man. More research suggests that women sometimes *invite* interruptions, at least in a business setting. Often, women share personal experiences when engaged in conversation, and that not only makes them appear warm and friendly, it also encourages others to open up. But too much storytelling—especially at work— can turn people (particularly men) off and lead them to interrupt you.

- **Women are emotional listeners.** Their body language and facial expressions when listening are far more animated than men's. That's because women like to connect with people they are talking to and feel the emotional message and undertones of a conversation. In fact, they are often far more concerned with the give-and-take of talking than the pertinent information discussed. On the flip side, men tend to be action-oriented listeners. They focus on listening to information pertinent to the task at hand. For example, if someone brings up a problem, the male brain will instantly begin to focus on potential solutions. By the way, action-oriented listeners typically have little patience for speakers who ramble off topic or include unnecessary details. So ladies, your takeaway tip here is that if you want a man to listen, cut to the chase and speak in bulleted points. Otherwise, he may tune you out.

- **Women listen "between the lines."** Because they rely on communication to connect with others and excel at reading others' body language, women are masters at picking up subtle hints about a speaker's mood and emotions and can almost always figure out what someone wants—even when that need or desire isn't expressed verbally. But men rarely possess this talent, which brings up another of my favorite hiccups when it comes to listening. I call it "the crystal ball effect," and ladies, I've never met a man that has one. In essence, because women can often read others' minds, they expect men to be able do the same.

If you're a woman in a romantic relationship, you know what I'm talking about. You have the notion that your man is so in tune with you, that he's able to "hear" what you want, need, and are struggling with, etc. without you having to spell it out. Yet, when he fails to pick up on all the hints you've dropped, he lands in the doghouse for not listening! Bottom line: If you want to be heard and understood, tell your man *exactly* what you mean or what you want.

• **Men often slip into "Mr. Fix-It" mode.** Another classic listening issue that often arises between men and women occurs when a woman wants to share details about her day or talk about what's happening at work. Maybe her boss has overloaded her, or she had a minor spat with a coworker. In response, her partner begins interrupting by trying to offer solutions to her "problems." Well guys, I have some great news for you...STOP! You're not expected to respond when your significant other is recapping her day. She just wants you to listen, and by doing so, you'll earn major brownie points. Oh, and by the way, if she *does* want your feedback or advice, she'll let you know. And if you're unsure about what she wants or needs from you, ask! If you want a billion brownie points, simply add, "Tell me more..." occasionally—and grab some popcorn!

Working on being "all ears" isn't easy, but it will pay huge dividends, at home, at work and with your family and friends. Hey, it worked out really well for Dumbo!

Chapter Four

READ THE SIGNS

Raise your hand if this sounds familiar: During a conversation with a colleague or a loved one, you notice their eyes shifting or rolling. Or you detect a distinctive change in their body posture. Or you notice their shoulders drop, their head tilt back or they turn slightly away. These are all signs that there's been a significant shift in attitude regarding your conversation.

Let's face it: We are always communicating, even when we're not speaking. That's because our voice, our demeanor, our tone and body language can speak volumes. It is a scientific fact that people's gestures give away their *true* intentions. Yet, most of us don't know how to read body language—and don't realize how our own physical movements speak to others. This chapter will discuss how our body language influences what others are thinking about us, as well as strategies for "speed reading" what others are saying to us through their body language.

As we discussed in the last chapter, listening is not a passive activity, and if you have the desire to revolutionize your relationships, then learning how to read the signs being given off by the people you are speaking with will make you a more masterful communicator. I don't care if you're speaking to family, friends, a loved one, in a business meeting, conducting an interview or hanging out in a social setting, you're constantly being bombarded with non-verbal messages. The question is, "Other than the obvious signs, are you picking up on the gestures, movements and little hints that can help you understand the message being sent?"

From research and years of experience, I've learned that non-verbal signals account for roughly 60 to 80 percent of the impact of a message, while vocal sounds (tone, inflection, sighs...etc.) make up 20 to 30 percent, and a mere 7 to 10 percent is words. That old cliché, "actions speak louder than words," is not only true, but it's been proven that the brain perceives and processes non-verbal messages faster than it does verbal messages. If that information isn't news to you, than this might be: In situations where the facial expressions, body posture, gestures and other body signals we exhibit conflict with our verbal message, listeners will almost always accept and take action on the non-verbal message we are sending.

From the time I was in my early twenties—much longer ago than I care to admit—I've always been fascinated with people watching. For several years I worked in various nightclub as a DJ and bartender (hey, I had to pay my way through school somehow) and was constantly entertained by watching people interact. Whether observing single people, married couples, coworkers, groups of men or groups of women, I was fascinated watching how they communicated non-verbally. Were they having a good time? Did they really enjoy being around each other? Were they flirting? Were they dialed in to the person they were speaking with, or did it seem they'd rather be anywhere else but in the conversation in which they found themselves?

Based on many years of studying communications, I've learned that since body language evolved before we began to speak, it's more natural and authentic than words and much harder to mask—mainly because so much of it is subconscious. Think about it: If you're going to have a conversation with someone, you may map out in your mind how you verbally want to deliver that message. Depending on the type of conversation, you may even practice it in your head until you feel comfortable with your delivery. But have you ever recalled a time when you thought about having a conversation with someone and rehearsed the gestures, movements and facial expressions you were going to incorporate into your talk? I didn't think so. Yet, it's those non-verbal messages that will always be received quicker and taken more to heart by the person with whom you are speaking than whatever words are coming out of your mouth.

It should come as no surprise that when it comes to non-verbal communication, there are gender differences. Overall, women tend to be more animated and expressive then men are. Experts attribute this in part to evolution. Our male ancestors may have evolved as more poker-faced because showing their emotions—especially fear, weakness or guilt—could be dangerous. On the other side of the cave, female ancestors may have benefited from emotional expression, specifically when it came to communicating with infants and toddlers.

Advantage: Women?

In 1975, a footnote in the *Virginia Law Review* suggested that perhaps women should be excluded from jury duty. Why? Because their skill at observing and interpreting nonverbal communication might make them excessively vulnerable to body language effects, interfering with the defendant's right to an independent and unbiased jury.

Nurture is likely a contributing factor as well. From the beginning, parents, teachers and peers tend to socialize girls to think about interpersonal relationships and to be responsive to others. Meanwhile, boys are often taught to "suck it up" and suppress their emotions. We typically see this in athletic situations, or on the playground. If a boy gets injured, he's often told, "Only sissies cry" or "Come on, be a man." As a result, boys grow up learning to internalize their emotions. On the flip side, little girls are often told, "I know it hurts...it's okay to cry" or "Ouch, here's a hug...everything will be okay."

Women also excel at reading body language, and this appears to be true worldwide. In 125 studies involving various cultures, boys and men were consistently less accurate in interpreting unspoken gestures, messages and facial expressions. Men also reacted less intensely to raw emotions. Let's turn back the clock to childhood for one potential cause for this. Remember, growing up, many of little girls' favorite games (playing house and with dolls) focus on connecting, communicating and socializing with one another. These types of interaction lead girls to develop more proficient people skills, as well as a "sixth sense" for interpreting others' body language. Favorite boys' games, on the other hand (cars, guns or sports) tend to be more action oriented and competitive with the focus on playing hard and winning at all costs. Consequently, they don't get as much practice at reading people.

Another slight advantage women have over men when it comes to "taking it all in" is that they have wider peripheral vision than men do. As nest defenders, women developed brain software that allowed them to receive an arc of at least 45 degrees clear vision to each side of the head and above and below the nose. In fact, most women's peripheral vision extends to almost 180 degrees. Men, on the other hand, have eyes that are generally larger than a woman's, but their brain software evolved to allow them to best see straight ahead and at long distances. In other words, his vision field works much like a pair of binoculars, in that it's more centered on what's directly in front of him and out ahead of him. This allowed the hunter to zero in on targets off in the distance and block out anything that might distract him from harvesting his prey.

Eye Candy

"Almost every man has been accused at some time or another of ogling the opposite sex, but few women receive the same complaint from men. Sex researchers everywhere report that women look at men's bodies as much as, and sometimes more than, men look at women's. Yet, women with their superior peripheral vision rarely get caught."

-Allan and Barbara Pease, *Why Men Don't Listen and Women Can't Read Maps*

Signs, Signs, Everywhere There's Signs

To decode the unspoken messages people are sending your way, you have to be able to read the signs and understand the meaning or message that's carried along with them. For instance we've all heard that crossed arms (closed body posture) means that someone's probably not really listening to you, doesn't agree with what you're saying or isn't comfortable with how the conversation is going. Conversely, someone who is listening to you with open arms, leaning slightly toward you, making consistent eye contact and smiling usually means that your message is being received, and the person is positively engaged in what you're saying. For guys, if a woman you're talking to is twirling her hair, leaning her head slightly to one side and has an open stance, she's either flirting with you or is very into your message.

And what about the non-verbal messages you're sending out? Body language can be an extremely effective tool in revolutionizing your relationships. On the plus side, it can help you help you reach your goals by giving you presence and charisma. But it can also work against you by undermining your credibility and causing others to misinterpret your message. Here are nine body language blunders to watch out for:

• **Smiling too much**. Studies show that women smile nearly twice as much as men do. Women even smile when nobody's around—like when they're watching TV, grabbing a bite to eat or listening to an audio book. Smiling can be a very powerful tool and a great asset when utilized at the right time. After all, a smile projects warmth, conveys a sense of confidence and can help establish rapport with others. But when a smile doesn't match your tone of voice or the message you're trying to convey, signals get crossed. For example, when you're debating an issue with a colleague or trying to convince a client to purchase a product or service you offer, you want to be taken seriously. But if you smile too much, your message could get "lost in translation." Research also reveals that inappropriate smiling can make you appear weak and unassertive—and more commonly for women than men—be misinterpreted as a sign of flirtatious behavior.

• **Listening like a statue.** Men are masters at keeping a "poker face," which can work to their advantage in many business situations—like serious negotiations. But in neutral or friendly discussions, this lack of emotion can spell trouble, since it signals—particularly to women—that you're bored, not listening or not understanding what's being said. In men, biology is usually to blame for "stone faced" body language. Remember, the objective of the male warrior when listening was to remain impassive so as not to betray his emotions. In essence, men's lack of visual emotion allows them to feel in control of any given situation. But guys, be aware that this can often come across as condescending to people with whom you're talking.

• **Improper dosage of eye contact**. We've already established that maintaining good eye contact is critical to being a good listener. Turns out, there are other advantages to mastering this body language skill. One study I found revealed that job applicants who engage in significant eye contact are seen as more dependable, confident and responsible. In another, only applicants who used above average amounts of eye contact were asked to come back for a second round of interviews. Generally speaking, women engage in more eye contact, primarily as a way to connect with others and let them know they're listening. But when talking to men who don't reciprocate, women often perceive this behavior as signs of disinterest, avoidance or dishonesty. This is one of women's top complaints about men, and I hear it all the time: "Why won't he look me in the eye when we're having a discussion?" Guys, take note...when you avoid eye contact with people you're talking to—particularly women—it not only makes them feel insignificant, they may also assume that you're not interested at all in what they have to say.

Blame It On Testosterone

Are you ready for this? It turns out that testosterone may have an impact on how men make eye contact. A group of scientists at Cambridge University filmed year-old children at play and recorded the amount of eye contact they made with their mothers, all of whom had undergone amniocentesis during pregnancy. Researchers looked at various social factors—like birth order and parental education, as well as the level of testosterone the child had been exposed to in the womb. The results were eye opening. The more testosterone the child had been exposed to, the less able they were to make eye contact at one year of age.

Keep in mind that good eye contract doesn't entail staring someone down. In fact, too much eye contact can be offensive, since prolonged staring can signal anger, challenge (just like animals in the wild) or sexual attraction. The rules for effective eye contact are simple. Keep your gaze steady and firm, but look away every few seconds to break the pattern of a constant stare.

• **Commanding too much (or not enough) space**. It's a fact that leaders command more space than others do. In one recent study where volunteers were asked to grade videotaped subjects, 80 percent considered those who used more space around them—by leaning forward, putting their elbows on a chair or table, keeping their palms open or appearing relaxed—as confident, intelligent and powerful. Generally speaking, men excel at pulling off this type of body language. In contrast, women have a tendency to hold their arms and legs close to their bodies and sit rigidly and relatively still. Unfortunately, this can make them appear less powerful, since those who shift their positions occasionally are perceived as more comfortable, confident and in charge.

While standing, men typically take a military type stance—both feet on the ground, legs spread, chest out, and chin up. This type of posture is associated with authority and sends the message, "I'm confident and in control." The typical female stance, however, more closely resembles the third ballet position: legs together, arms held somewhat tightly to the body and the head sometimes slightly bowed. This posture is not so powerful; in fact, it can make women appear unsure of themselves and, even worse, submissive! Women can and should assume many of the relaxed positions that men typically do. Their legs don't have to be welded together and they should definitely stand, chin up, and take command.

Note to men: It's important to be aware of the impact your position can have on those around you. For instance, men often go into a meeting, and when seated, will put their hands behind their heads, lean back in their chair and "claim their ground." (I've got to admit that I've done this many times myself). The non-verbal message that's being broadcast here is, "I'm running this show" or "I'm one of the 'big dogs' here." However, others—particularly women—are generally put off by this type of sprawling posture and perceive it as arrogance. It can also backfire by creating an unnecessary barrier to communication.

• **Distracting or overpowering hand gestures.** (And I'm not talking about the obvious one that comes to mind here.). Studies show that women use twice the number of hand gestures that men do. Being expressive is a great tool, but if overused, it can become distracting, make you appear nervous and lessen the impact of your message. Many women have a tendency to "hand dance" during conversation—using gestures and movements from the elbows to the fingertips to emphasize points they're trying to make. They also tend to gesture more toward the body rather than away from it. But studies show these types of gestures can make women look smaller and appear less important. A better idea might be to emulate men—who tend to use larger sweeping gestures that move away from the body—as these are generally perceived as powerful. Men are also prone to finger pointing, which many consider to be rude, making this a no-no for both sexes.

• **Fidgeting.** It's hard not to fidget when you're feeling stressed or nervous. And many of us get ants in our pants when we're forced to sit through boring presentations or long, drawn-out meetings. Fidgeting can run the gamut from playing with your hair or wringing your hands, to tapping your pen on the table to fiddling with your watch or other jewelry. But beware that by using this kind of body language, you're sending a signal that you're bored, not interested in what's being said and lack control. Also, studies show that if you frequently touch your face while speaking, you could be perceived as lying.

• **Rubbing people the wrong way.** The power of touch is undeniable, and when carried out correctly, can create a wonderful bond between two people. Of course, physical contact at home is a critical component to staying connected with your significant other, but physical contact at work demands discretion.

There are some interesting studies about physical contact in the workplace. One, conducted by the School of Hotel Administration at Cornell University, showed that when restaurant servers touched their customers—even for as long as four seconds—they increased their tips by more than three percent. Other studies reveal that powerful people do more touching then powerless people do, possibly because it's easier for them to get away with it. And when researcher Nancy Henly looked at non-verbal behavior in Fortune 500 companies, she found that touch among men tends to be more acceptable with authority and is a signal of status.

Regarding gender and touch, it's definitely a matter of different strokes for different folks. Research reveals that women tend to rely on touch to soothe, connect or bond with others, while men use physical interaction to assert status or power. Caution: At work, both sexes need to be careful about touching on the job. Even a subtle touch by a woman can be misinterpreted by a man as flirting—and the same holds true for a man touching a woman. Even more serious, inappropriate touching can be grounds for sexual harassment and could potentially lead to termination. To be safe, adopt a hands–off policy at work, and always remind yourself that, when in doubt, keep your hands in your pockets.

• **Misunderstanding silence.** A short pause in a conversation isn't a green light for you to pick up where the other person left off. The silence could indicate that the person you're talking to doesn't understand what you've just said. It may mean they need a moment to let your words sink in, or they may simply need a few seconds to formulate a response. Whatever the reason for the "conversation time–out," both men and women can benefit from learning how to use silence as a power tool. Most experts will tell you that when you're talking business, trying to close a deal or negotiate a contract, "whoever talks first, typically loses." So, look for opportunities to use powerful pauses and moments of silence to your advantage.

• **Showing too much emotion.** When a man shows emotion—even shedding some tears—people tend to think it's touching, sweet, sensitive and caring. When a woman cries, however, she's often viewed as being emotionally liable. There's no question that men struggle when women cry, especially at work. In fact, they will often conclude that she can't handle the pressures of her job. That's because tears at work chip away at a woman's authority and can make her appear weak, not in control of her emotions and even slightly irrational.

Surveys show that anger and frustration are generally the root cause of women's tears. Men are allowed to be more direct and can vent in multiple ways—pounding a table, raising their voice, or acting out in some non–threatening physical manner. But women are expected to be more passive. There's no question that emotional outbursts at work can have an impact on your professional image, and perhaps the best way for both men and women to "let it all out" is privately—and behind closed doors.

Improve Your Marriage Without Saying a Word

A lot of the information we've discussed thus far in this chapter has centered around body language at work. But what about non-verbal communication at home? Staying connected with the love of your life can be a challenge, and with so many demands on your time, it's imperative that you maximize the together time you have. It's a no-brainer that setting aside time every day to communicate verbally helps keep you stay connected, but nonverbal communication can also go a long way in cementing your romantic relationships. I recommend:

- **Touching each other often.** If you didn't learn this off-the-wall factoid in high school science class here it is: the skin is the largest organ of the human body, measuring two square yards. From birth, girls are dramatically more sensitive to touch, and as we established earlier, in adulthood, a woman's skin is at least ten times more sensitive to touch and pressure than a man's. So guys, use this information to your advantage and touch your lady often. Keep in mind that it doesn't always have to be a big bear hug. A gentle brush or a soft squeeze as you walk past her, a soft kiss on the cheek or even pressing your body up against hers are all powerful ways of communicating. And ladies, giving your man a shoulder rub or a kiss on the neck always feels good.

- **Never stop flirting.** Ladies, you know how to tilt your head and flash that special smile that lets your man know how much you love him. And guys, don't hesitate to use your "come and get me" look or stance when she isn't expecting it. Be spontaneous and mix up the ways you choose to be affectionate. Also, get creative by being mindful of not repeating the same behaviors and gestures.

- **Being in tune with his/her mood.** Given our crazy schedules, it's sometimes hard to set aside our worries, fears, concerns and emotions long enough to check in with how our partner is doing. What's more, sometimes even when we ask, we may get a quick (and unrevealing), "Fine" in response. The thing is, you don't even need to ask—just pay attention—since your significant other is constantly giving off nonverbal cues about how he/she is doing. Watch for long periods of silence, lack of eye contact, slumped shoulders, walking around with a slightly bowed head or your significant other frequently seeking a place to "hide" and avoid talking. I always encourage the clients I work with to "rally" at some point every day to gauge what's happening with your partner, and if you sense something is not right, try initiating a discussion or expressing affection nonverbally. A little attention can go a long way in turning a person's day around and putting a smile on their face—as well as yours.

• **Walking together.** This may seem pretty basic, but studies show that emotionally connected couples almost always walk side-by-side and even hold hands (crazy concept, I know). In fact, one partner walking ahead or behind the other is often a non-verbal clue that someone has something on his/her mind that they're not talking about, or he/she may be upset.

• **Making frequent eye contact.** This one falls into the "no-brainer" category. Whether at home or in a social setting, happy couples will frequently make eye contact as a manner of just checking in to see if everything is okay. So, make sure you're glancing across the room every so often to let your partner know that you're in tune with him/her. And during more romantic moments, gaze into the eyes of the one you love and let them peer deep into your soul so they can see how much they mean to you.

In Sync

It only makes sense that if you spend a great deal of time with a person, you'll often begin to pick up on some of the same mannerisms, gestures and movements. In fact, studies indicate that couples that are in love even have heart rates that are in perfect synchronization.

- **Paying attention to seating arrangements.** When you and your significant other are in the same room, where you sit as couple often speaks volumes about the status of your relationship. For instance, research reveals that newlyweds often sit right next to each other—and almost never across the room. As relationships mature, this dynamic often softens a bit, but it's always worth paying attention to. If the status of your relationship is good, your partner should be close by.

- **Connecting daily.** Happy couples find ways to connect with each other on a daily basis, and I'll talk more about this in Chapter Seven. This is extremely important, as it relates to the health of your relationship. When reuniting at the end of the day, do you immediately hug or kiss each other? Do you often hold hands when out in public? Is there frequent eye contact, and do you touch each other often? If there are problems bubbling below the surface, physical interaction and the amount of time spent together diminishes. Be mindful of the status of your relationship and take action if you're concerned it isn't in a healthy place. Fender-bender car accidents are often easily fixed, but head-on collisions can result in a total loss.

- **Watching your body language in the bedroom.** Much more on this to come, but pay attention to what's happening in your love life by learning to "read the signs." Does your partner pull you closer when you're kissing? Do their hands wander freely as if they're trying to consume every inch of you? What sounds do they make (or not make) as you progress through a lovemaking session? Being in tune in the bedroom is like listening to an orchestra playing in perfect harmony...you just feel so relaxed and alive as the final note floats past you.

Chapter Five

TOUGH CONVERSATIONS MADE EASY

We've all been there: We know we must confront a coworker, client, friend or significant other about some type of sticky situation. We assume the encounter will be uncomfortable, so we often put it off in hopes the problem will: (a) go away or (b) somehow take care of itself. Or, we repeatedly mull it over until we can no longer delay the inevitable and then finally stumble through the confrontation. Maybe we feel we deserve a raise or promotion at work but can't bring ourselves to ask for it. Maybe we have to reprimand an employee we're fond of or need to confront a coworker who took credit for our idea. Or, maybe we're struggling to find a way to motivate our significant other to change an annoying behavior.

How to have tough conversations with anyone—and with less stress and more success? And what's the best way to handle conflict, which is inevitable in any relationship? Keep reading...

"I Don't Know How To Say This..."

Does anyone really look forward to having tough conversations? I know I don't. For some, the task is almost unbearable. Stress levels rise, blood pressure goes up and the thought of what might go wrong or how badly feelings will be hurt is almost too much to handle. If all of this sounds familiar, you're far from alone. According to a survey conducted by experts at Development Dimensions International, 20.4 percent of employees surveyed said they loathed having difficult conversations with their bosses more than:

(a) receiving a speeding ticket
(b) catching a cold
(c) paying taxes
(d) doing housework
(e) getting a credit card bill.

Initiating a tough conversation is never a fun thing to do, but it is often a necessary evil. The key to handling it successfully involves understanding the issue, then taking action to help solve the problem. Oh, and keep in mind that procrastinating doesn't pay. In fact, if you can bite the bullet and force yourself to speak up *before* things get out of hand, you'll definitely minimize the intensity of the talk.

Whether the tough conversation you need to have is with a boss, employee, coworker, friend, family member or significant other, follow these tips to keep your discussion productive and positive, regardless of your topic:

• **Give a heads up.** Avoid blindsiding someone you need to have a tough conversation with. Surprise is a tactic better left for war than building a team or strengthening a relationship with a coworker or loved one. And instead of saying, "We need to talk," which tends to send most folks into panic mode, try less intimidating phrases like, "I'd like to get your opinion on...," "I'd like to talk to you about...," "I'd like to get your perspective regarding..." or "It's really important to me if we could take a few minutes to talk about..." Finally, confront the person you need to have a tough conversation with privately instead of in front of others (coworkers, fellow team members, kids, in-laws, etc.). Otherwise, they're certain to become defensive, and your conversation will have no chance at being constructive.

Important: If the tough conversation you need to have is with a colleague or coworker with whom you have a contentious relationship, you might not be the top choice to offer advice or feedback regarding their performance or job effectiveness. In cases like this, consider "delegating" the task to someone with whom the person has a more amicable relationship. That way, he/she will be much more receptive.

• **Set the stage.** You've heard the old adage that there's a time and place for everything, and this is particularly true when discussing sensitive topics. Have your sit-down in a place that's private, quiet and free of distractions—and if the conversation is happening at work, don't initiate a dialogue when phones are ringing off the hook or important deadlines are looming. Make sure the person with whom you're speaking isn't tired, hungry or in a bad mood when you talk to him/her. As a rule of thumb, I've found the best time to have tough conversations is mid-morning. Delaying discussions until close to quitting time or sitting down to have a heart-to-heart talk with your significant other within minutes after you both get home from work probably isn't a good idea.

• **Watch where you sit.** For one-on-one conversations—especially those with emotional potential—sitting in opposite-facing positions creates a feeling of confrontation. Sitting across a table or desk adds even more of a barrier to the conversation and can increase tension, plus make the person you're talking to feel insecure and defensive. If possible, try to sit at a diagonal angle of about 45 degrees, as this sets a more friendly, equitable tone. Be mindful not to place chairs so close together that personal space feels invaded, but don't sit too far apart, either. The goal is to build feelings of cooperation and trust.

• **Try to start and end with a quick compliment.** This is a great way to frame your talk and lets the other person know this isn't an inquisition and that you're not just focused on discussing negative behavior or performance. Find something positive to say about them from the get go, as this will make them more receptive to hearing what you have to say. Try to end your conversation on a positive note, too, so the person won't walk away feeling like a failure.

I once had to initiate a tough conversation with Jason, an employee I managed. He was one of my favorites, and his customer service work was exemplary, but his sales process needed to be fine-tuned. He was great at telling the company story to potential customers, but he had a tendency to delve so deeply into that part of his presentation, that it often took too long for him to get to the pitch—which frequently resulted in losing the sale. I initiated my conversation with Jason by complimenting him on his ability to connect with customers and provide top-notch customer service. That enabled him to relax, making it easier for me to address the issue of him needing to tighten up his sales presentation. Once he understood that taking those steps would ultimately result in increased sales—and more commission for him—he was eager to fine-tune his presentation. I wrapped our conversation up with another compliment—telling him that, given his product knowledge and his knack for connecting with clients, this challenge would be a relatively easy transition for him to make. He agreed.

• **But get to the point.** To avoid making tough conversations even more tense, skip the small talk. Beating around the bush just doesn't work when you're attempting to alter behavior or change routines. So, be honest and direct by stating—then describing—what's on your mind, what's bugging you, or simply what you'd like to see changed. Then ask for what you want. Having a discussion is great, but at some point you need to communicate exactly what it is that you're asking the person to do. Is it being more punctual? Is it spending more time with the kids? Is it being more attentive to you? Spell it out.

• **Check your delivery.** In your eagerness to get the conversation out of the way, be careful about how you sound. Does your voice have an edge to it, or does it carry a demanding tone that could make your listener feel defensive? If need be, take a deep breath before delivering your message, then do it in a calm, non threatening manner.

• **Look the person in the eye**. Granted, this can be challenging to pull off when you're having a tough conversation with someone, but making eye contact not only communicates sincerity, it's also critical to keeping you both focused on the conversation. Looking the other person in the eye will also enable you to read his/her body language, which can provide you with valuable clues about how the discussion is going.

• **Listen for feedback.** This is where you take everything you learned in Chapter Four and put it to work for you. Pay attention to the nonverbal cues the other person is giving off and use what you're "hearing" to determine how to proceed with the conversation. If they're becoming agitated or consistently more vocal, it may be time to take a short break or schedule your discussion to continue at another time.

• **Don't make it personal.** Keep the conversation focused on behaviors or habits you want to change, not the individual's character. This way, you're more likely to get the person to buy into your suggestions— and you're far more likely to see positive results. Remember, feedback is not about insulting someone; it's about telling him or her how to improve and excel. For example, you would never say to an employee you supervise, "Hiring you was a big mistake." Instead, you would say, "You've been making quite a few mistakes that we need to work on." Don't speak "at" or "down" to the person, as this signals a lack of respect. Besides, nobody enjoys being humiliated, feeling stupid or thinking that they're being treated like a child.

• **Take a "we're in this together" approach.** Ask questions like, "What do you think we can do to solve this problem?" or "How can we work together to improve this situation?" It's always beneficial to make the individual feel like you're tackling a problem together. This will also help strengthen your bond and likely result in the person making the desired changes more quickly, since it will feel like they have someone supporting their efforts.

• **Use gentle humor when appropriate.** Depending on the severity of the discussion, you may find a window of opportunity to interject some humor. If it feels right (and be cautious here) to toss in a little humor with your message, this can be a powerful tool that lightens the mood of the conversation. Studies show that when used appropriately, humor won't diminish the seriousness of the feedback you're giving. In fact, it can actually help the person on the receiving end open up and take in what you're saying without feeling so defensive. It's important to know the person fairly well before applying this technique, however, as the last thing you want is for them to think the situation is a joke to you.

• **Wrap things up with a question.** Once you've delivered your message, expressed your concerns and discussed moving forward, ask the person you're addressing if he/she has any questions or ideas on how to carry out the new goals you've set. So often people resist change because they just don't think they're being heard. This is where "listening" plays a huge role. Hearing the other person out gives him/her a chance to vent and release pent-up emotions and frustrations.

When You're In The Hot Seat

How should you respond when *you* are on the receiving end of a tough conversation? Here's what I recommend:

• **Watch your body language.** You may not like what you're hearing, but try to stay calm and show you're listening. This means maintaining eye contact and avoiding closed body language, like crossing your arms.

• **Don't play defense.** Take what's being said to you as *constructive* criticism and a way for you to be a better employee, manager, friend or spouse. Unless there are valid reasons to do so, avoid trying to justify behaviors that the person who's talking to you finds unacceptable, and instead of blaming others, take responsibility for your actions and verbally commit to improving.

• **Make sure you understand the problem.** When the discussion is over, ask questions and then rephrase the issue: "As I understand it, you are concerned about...and you would like me to (state solution). Is that correct?"

• **Ask for a checkup.** Request a follow-up meeting to discuss progress or improvement. This offers proof that you're a team player and value the speaker's input and feedback.

The Dreaded "C" Word

In this instance, "C" stands for conflict, which is inevitable in any relationship. Most people view conflict as negative or destructive and having an effect similar to that of termites in eroding the foundation of our relationships. In fact, many of us go out of our way to avoid it. Big mistake. Handled properly, conflict—whether it occurs at work or at home—can create positive changes by:

• Facilitating growth

• Fostering the exchange of ideas and information

• Increasing camaraderie among coworkers

• Creating an energetic work environment

• Boosting productivity

• Improving communication

• Decreasing feelings of animosity

• Bolstering feelings of trust and support

"Fight or Flight" vs. "Tend and Befriend"

Successful, productive and harmonious male-female relationships depend on couples and coworkers being able to handle conflict—whether it occurs in the boardroom or the bedroom. Have you ever heard a story about two guys getting so mad at each other that they decide to settle their argument with a fist fight? Yet, after a display of "macho" behavior, and in the aftermath of a few punches, the "winner" will sometimes offer to buy the "loser" a drink. Literally moments later, they can be seen acting like long-time buddies and making light of their recent altercation. Granted, this isn't always the outcome of male-to-male confrontations, but if we're all going to become better at solving conflict, we need to understand how men and women typically approach and deal with it.

For men, stressful situations, such as major disagreements, have been shown to make them want to put up their dukes or disappear into their caves. The first response is purely physical and happens because when men feel threatened, they experience a sudden increase in testosterone and adrenaline. This hormonal jolt is accompanied by an increase in blood pressure and heart rate, and since it's difficult for them to turn down the thermostat, feelings of aggression take over. Not to say that aggression always involves a fistfight, but at the very least, a man who feels threatened will likely lash out.

Or he will disappear into his cave and wait for the storm to pass—which is the typical psychological response men have to conflict. Amazingly, upon their return, they may even act as if nothing happened! What gives? Men usually do this because they have no clue how to respond to personal conflict, so they stop communicating altogether out of fear of saying something wrong, hurtful or running the risk of looking like a fool.

I can relate. I remember earlier in my life getting into some major arguments with my parents, friends, bosses or girlfriends just because I felt like I was being attacked. If I didn't escalate the conversation I would often remove myself from the situation and seek sanctity in the nearest "cave" I could find until I was able to settle down. It took years for me to understand that I was part of the problem, and that the people I was in conflict with were just trying to address various concerns that would result in a more productive and stronger relationship. So guys, please pause for a minute here and understand that conflict does not always equal personal attack.

On the flip side, women, who by nature are problem solvers, tend to think and talk their way through conflict. Doing this makes them feel better and helps keep them calm. Women tend also tend to be more obliging and accommodating than men when resolving conflict—often demonstrating what researchers call "soothing" behaviors that cater to the needs and desires of the other person, sometimes at the expense of their own happiness.

Not to say that women aren't aggressive or don't have their own version of "disappearing into the cave." They just tend to be more subtle about it. For example, an angry woman will sometimes give a man the silent treatment or the cold shoulder. And while certainly not immune to emotional outbursts, women typically attempt to keep their emotions in check until the conflict is resolved. Have you ever been around a woman that appears to keep her cool during a conflict, but once it's over, the emotion begins pouring out?

Can't We All Just Get Along?

Regardless of gender, the obvious solution is to face conflict head on and discuss issues as soon as possible. You don't have to get into a heated argument, defend yourself or even try to solve the problem. You just need to be open to laying everything out on the table, and allowing the other person to do the same so you can clear the air and get back to normal.

You also need to master the art of fighting fairly, and here are some tips on how to do that:

• **Be clear but cordial.** What do you want to change or see changed? Say it, then briefly discuss the benefits it will bring to the relationship. Also, when voicing complaints, be sure to attack the *problem*, not the person. After dating for three years, Stephanie and Rick sought my help because they were constantly arguing about jealousy issues. Rick would often check out other women, which infuriated Stephanie, and when she'd accuse him of being a "pig," Rick would get pissed. I finally convinced Stephanie to let Rick "be a man." I explained to her that men are visual creatures, and that while we appreciate looking at pretty women, it doesn't mean we want to be with them. Once Stephanie realized that Rick was with her because he loved her, she felt enlightened. Stephanie still gets a little jealous when Rick's eyes wander, but both agree they've made a lot of progress, and their arguments involving jealousy are fewer and far between.

• **Establish ground rules.** Verbal disagreements are settings ripe for interruptions, which can only turn up the anger meter. So, make sure each of you has time to express your feelings. Whether you use a kitchen timer or a stopwatch, establish either a 2 and 2 or 3 and 3. This means the person talking has the floor for either two or three minutes while the other person waits for his or her turn to speak, and there are no interruptions until each person's time is up. This sounds so simple, but I've seen it work miracles. If you don't want to use a timing system, then use an object. Remember the earlier story I shared about Sean and Abby and their stuffed penguin? Whoever was holding the stuffed penguin had the floor. Try it.

• **Put "I" before "we"...at least initially.** Start the discussion using "I" statements. This avoids assigning blame or making the other person feel like you're telling them what they think, believe or want (which feels controlling and invites defensiveness). Instead, focus on identifying your *own* unmet needs. Explain how you feel, then give examples of *why* you feel that way. Later, once you start discussing potential solutions to your problem, switch to "we" mode to evoke a "we're-in-this-together" team approach.

• **Remain in the present.** Tossing out phrases like, "You always" and "you never" don't belong in your arguments. Bringing up history indicates to the other person that nothing will ever change, so why bother trying to find solutions to problems? And when discussing hot topics, deal with a single issue at a time—and only what's happened that day to set things off. Resist the urge to rehash old issues that happened six months or a year ago, as doing this will only cloud the issue at hand.

• **Broaden your outlook.** Try and see the *whole* picture, not just your own point of view. For many of us, the tendency in conflict is to protect ourselves, but that often means damaging the relationship in the long haul.

• **Language, please!** Avoid ridiculing, name-calling and swearing. Aggressive use of language sends the message that you're trying to control the conversation, and when that happens, the other person is bound to tune you out. No matter how right you may be, you don't want the people you're arguing with to become so busy thinking about how to defend themselves that they don't hear a word you're saying. Besides, having discussions isn't about controlling the conversation, anyway. It's all about addressing problems and concerns—and ultimately finding ways to improve your relationship.

• **Brainstorm possibilities.** Nothing is more important than coming out of a discussion with a resolution and new plan of action, so focus on coming up with as many solutions as you can, then pick the one that works best for *both* of you. Above all, be willing to compromise. Remember, conflicts aren't about winning or losing; the best resolutions have some type of win-win component.

• **Know when to put yourselves in time-out.** If your discussion gets too heated, or if either (or both) of you is growing increasingly agitated, and there's no resolution in sight, hit the pause button and take a short break to cool off, calm down and gain perspective. Use this time-out to reflect on why you feel the way you do and to focus on how to express yourself in a positive way. Take time to ponder the other person's feelings and point of view, too.

Studies show that a time-out should last at least 30 minutes, since it takes at least that long for your body to return to a normal resting state and for your thoughts to become less hostile or defensive. What's more once you've both had a chance to calm down, chances are you'll be pleasantly surprised at how different your outlook can be—and how much quicker you'll progress at resolving your issue.

It's Okay To Agree to Disagree

It's impossible for two people to see eye-to-eye on *everything*, and sometimes the best way to resolve conflict is to call a truce and agree to disagree. This strategy doesn't mean you're throwing in the towel or giving up on something that's important to you. It's more about realizing that there are simply some behaviors in others you cannot change, and rather than repeatedly arguing about them, it's healthier just to accept them. Granted, this is often easier said than done, but by agreeing to disagree, you send a powerful message to each other: that you have enough self-respect and respect for the other person to let it go.

• **Get help if you need it.** As much I'd like to think that all conflicts—both professional and personal—can be solved by the parties involved, the reality is that sometimes we need help from someone who's unbiased. A mediator can be a mutual friend, a boss, a minister, a counselor or a psychologist. Many of us are reluctant to seek help and guidance because doing so makes us feel weak or even embarrassed. Don't even go there. In my opinion, asking for help at either solving a problem or attempting to patch up a relationship demonstrates the highest level of maturity and commitment possible. And don't wait until your relationship with someone is in crisis to put out an SOS call to a mediator. It's much harder to recover from an "emergency state" than it is to nip problems in the bud early on.

Go to Bed Angry!

Your parents may have advised against this, but staying up all night to finish an argument is never a good idea. Once the "fight or flight" system kicks in, there's no switch to turn it off, so the longer your debate continues, the more emotional things will get and the more likely you'll both keep adding fuel to the blaze. Put the brakes on, get some sleep, and set a time to revisit the issue. Otherwise, one or both of you will end up saying things you truly don't mean—and those words could be very damaging to your relationship.

• **Look ahead.** Problems aren't properly resolved until both parties in the argument feel better about the situation and reassured that the issue won't be revisited again and again. So, set guidelines for how to handle a similar situation in the future. You might say something like, 'Let's commit that you will let me know right away if I do something that upsets you, and when you bring it to my attention, we will stop what we are doing to address it."

The Importance of Being Earnest

Once conflict has been resolved, it may be time for one (or maybe both) of you to clear the air with an apology. Apologies are critical to strong, happy and productive relationships, yet studies confirm what most of us have long known: that many of us have trouble saying we're sorry. FYI, research also reveals that men apologize 30 percent less than women do.

What's so important about saying I'm sorry? For starters, these three little words have amazing powers to heal rifts and diminish stress in a relationship, eliminate grudges and generate forgiveness. An apology validates the other person's feelings, helps us move past our anger and goes a long way at preventing further misunderstandings. What's more, while an apology can't undo harmful past actions, if uttered sincerely and effectively, it *can* undo the negative effects of those actions.

When Someone Tells You They're Sorry

Ever wondered why hearing those words feels so good? Research shows that receiving an apology has a noticeable, positive physical effect on the body. Blood pressure decreases, heart rate slows and breathing becomes steadier.

To Err is Human, To Forgive is Divine

Forgiving others when you feel you've been wronged ranks right up there with apologies, both in terms of how important this step is to restoring your relationships and how challenging it can often be to pull off. But the thing is, if you continue to hold on to things that happened in the past, you're only punishing *yourself,* since clinging to anger and resentment will only make your own life miserable. Regardless of who you feel has "done you wrong"—be it your boss, a coworker, a parent, your child or your significant other, forgiving them is the only way to make peace and move on to reestablishing a strong and productive relationship.

I'm not saying you have to forget, because you may never be able to do that. But you can (and should) choose to forgive and move on. Remember, forgiveness is not something you do for someone else; it's a gift you give to *yourself.* And the benefits you reap in return—peace of mind, plus healthier and happier relationships all around—are well worth it!

Chapter Six

SUNNY SIDE UP

A nd I'm not talking about how you order your eggs for breakfast, although personally, a couple of sunny side up eggs with a few pancakes to start your day never seems like a bad idea. But as your day transitions from breakfast to work and life, I have a question for you: "How successful are you in taking your 'sunny side up' disposition from the breakfast table to the office and back home to your family?" With the demands of life that each and every one of us faces on a daily basis, having or maintaining a positive attitude and state of mind has become more and more challenging.

Negativity seems to impact, take over, affect our day and have the ability to change our mood more often that positive events. In fact, pay close attention to when you go to work or find yourself in a social setting, and it won't take long to notice how complaining or negative conversations have become an integral part of our daily routines. "We use complaints as icebreakers," observes Robin Kowalski, Ph.D., a professor of psychology at Clemson University. "We start a conversation with a negative observation because we know that will get us a bigger response than saying something positive would."

Are the work and home environments we live in really that bad? Or does it have more to do with the way we choose to process the events of the day? Considering how we communicate and how others communicate with us, does that have us staring at a glass that's half empty? Personally, I believe it's a combination of both how we deal with situations mentally and how we communicate. The most effective communicators are positive communicators. At work, their can-do spirit earns accolades from superiors and is often contagious among subordinates and colleagues. At home, their "we-can-work-this-out" attitude makes them more lovable and approachable. Unfortunately, staying positive in a world full of negative influences and an abundance of naysayers can be challenging. This chapter will discuss the elements of positive communication and provide tips on how to be "like a duck" by learning to let negativity roll off of you just like water rolls off a duck's back.

The Power of Praise and Compliments

Mark Twain once said, "I can live a whole month on one compliment." And while that may have been true for Mr. Twain back in the day, times have changed just a bit. Nevertheless, his philosophy still holds true in today's professional and domestic arenas. The effect compliments can have on the human psyche is indisputable. Almost drug-like, the sensation one feels when they're being complimented can often heighten or change the momentum of their day.

Starving For Appreciation

A recent Gallup Poll revealed that a whopping 65 percent of Americans said they had not received recognition in the

> past year. And according to a U.S. Department of Labor Study, the number one reason people leave organizations is that they don't feel appreciated.

In fact, there's even scientific data that supports how effective compliments are. Check this out: When you give a compliment to someone, they actually experience a joyful boost of energy. And according to Monica Strobel, author of *The Compliment Quotient,* here's how it works: As the person receives the compliment, "an endorphin rush accompanies the physical changes of turning up the edges of our mouth and crinkling our cheeks and eyes—or what we know as a smile," she explains. "In turn, the vibrational exchange with your compliment jump-starts your nerve endings, like that smile or a bit of good humor, which releases the feel-good chemical, serotonin."

Compliments not only make people feel good, they communicate that you're in tune with others and paying attention to what's going on in their lives. After all, each of us likes to feel special. Compliments are also a great tool to use as a conversation starter. Think about it...when's the last time someone gave you a compliment, and you responded by terminating the conversation? I'm guessing never. So, if you have a relationship—either at home or at work—that could use a boost, try complimenting the person and then pay attention to how that individual responds to you.

Flattery WILL Get You Everywhere!

Studies show that people who compliment others on a regular basis are perceived as positive and often attract a higher frequency of attention from family, friends, coworkers and significant others. In my earlier professional days I remember being managed by people who ruled by fear and doled out very few compliments. I spent most of my time concentrating on not screwing up and spent very little time thinking about how I could do my job better—or what I could learn that would make me a more effective employee. It wasn't until I became a manager that I began to realize that if I praised my staff on a regular basis, their attitudes, productivity and willingness to go above and beyond began to show.

What is about compliments and praise that can turn an unhappy environment into a healthy one? Right off the top, people who feel they're appreciated, valued and respected are more motivated then those who think nobody is watching or cares about what they do. They're more in tune and engaged in what they do, and they're more invested and committed to the team and organization, because they know they're making a difference. That's extremely important when working in a company where budgets are tight and financial rewards aren't possible.

There is no question that responsibility equals more pressure. Supervisors have more pressure than basic staff, General Managers have more pressure than supervisors, and District Managers have more pressure than GMs—and so on all the way up the chain until you reach ownership. Successful individuals and companies have learned that crap doesn't have to roll downhill.

If you want to be successful and have your staff and upper management respect you, learn to shoulder the responsibilities you have by using positive feedback to build a team that's willing to work hard and go the extra mile for you. We all struggle these days with creating balance in our lives, and individually, we all have responsibilities that weigh on our minds. The last thing any of us wants to do is increase the level of negative influences and events in our day. No matter what position you have in your profession—and we'll talk about personal relationships later in this chapter—you can have a huge influence on the environment you work in by looking for opportunities to compliment those you come in contact with.

When Darren, an executive at a major advertising firm in Houston, came to me, he was worried about losing his job. In a downsized economy, competition for clients was intensifying, but he was having trouble motivating his staff to go the extra mile. Darren had not been much of a hands-on manager, but once he started getting to know his staff better, he was able to dole out genuine compliments to them—on their performance, their work ethic, their problem-solving abilities and even their appearance. As a result, his team grew closer and felt motivated to work harder. The end result? Commissions doubled in a six-month period.

The Best Way to Dish Out Compliments

The joy of giving compliments is that it doesn't take much effort, and it can quickly turn you into a "people magnet." But this works only if you do it correctly:

• **Be specific.** Praise that's vague can make a bad impression and will have little to no effect on the receiver. Saying, "Thanks everybody, you did a great job," is all well and good, but try giving it a more laser-type approach—as in, "Thanks everybody for the time, thought, and energy you put into our client's new ad campaign. They're already seeing results and couldn't be happier." Elaborating allows those you're praising to absorb the feedback and take ownership of the role they played.

• **Praise people behind their backs.** We're all familiar with the concept of people talking behind our backs, which can be poisonous to working relationships. But try flipping this around and using the same concept with compliments. The news will eventually circle back around to the person you praised, and they'll know you thought highly enough about them to share your thoughts with others. Example: "Hey John, Dave was telling me you did a terrific job on the XYZ project...way to go!" This may sound a little corny, but I'm telling you it works.

• **Match the quality of the praise to the difficulty of the task.** If an assigned task was relatively simple and easy, then a quick "Thanks so much for helping out with that," or, "Hey, that's perfect," is appropriate. But if the task was larger and more complicated, consider pulling a person aside whose efforts stood out and having a brief discussion about how well he/she performed. And if it took a group effort to complete a difficult task or assignment, in addition to offering words of praise, don't' hesitate to do something special for the group—like treating them to lunch or offering some other token of appreciation. Praise does to the soul what water does to our bodies...it keeps us healthy, refreshed and motivated to continue doing a good job.

• **Praise the everyday little stuff along with the exceptional.** Noticing an outstanding effort is like hitting someone in the face with a pie: you can't miss the after-effects. But showing those around you that you appreciate even the small, routine everyday tasks and duties that are being recognized is huge. Your positive feedback will directly impact the atmosphere, mood and motivation levels of your staff. One particularly interesting aspect about praise is the chemical reaction it causes in its receivers. Research shows that when we hear something we like, a burst of dopamine is released in our brains. Dopamine is a neurotransmitter associated with feelings of joy, pride, satisfaction and well-being.

• **Put it in writing.** Send an email or hand-write a quick note of thanks. This makes compliments even more special because the recipient can read—and re-read—your kind words of praise.

• **Avoid praising while simultaneously asking for a favor.** I've seen it done, and trust me when I tell you that it negates the praise altogether. In fact, it can make your praise seem like a setup for whatever you're asking for.

Turn A Bad Day Into a Great One

While doling out more compliments is a great way to improve relationships with colleagues and coworkers, controlling your own state of mind and choosing to dwell on the positive is equally important—and can go a long way in increasing the quality of your life, both at work and at home. Frustrations, and negative events happen to most of during the course of the day. It could be something as simple as your significant other waking up on the wrong side of the bed and picking a fight with you first thing, an encounter with a rude driver during your commute to the office, a client leaving you an angry voice mail or your boss chewing you out for making a mistake. I've heard story after story about how people allow negative events that happen in the first few hours of their day completely mess up the rest of their day.

The great news is, if you have the desire, you can train yourself to reduce the impact negative events have on your day. Here's how:

• **Make it temporary.** When something negative happens in your day, allow yourself to feel and experience all of the emotions associated with the event, but don't let it control you the rest of the day. A great technique is to set a time limit on how long you can be upset, angry, irritated or frustrated. For instance, if you and your supervisor have a disagreement, and that conversation has affected you emotionally, tell yourself, "I'm really mad at my boss, but I'm only going to let it affect me for fifteen minutes, and then I'm moving on with my day." It's never a good idea to bottle up emotions because, chances are, they'll bubble beneath the surface and have a negative effect on you for the remainder of the day anyway. So often—and I've experienced this myself—a single bad event can snowball into a day you struggle to get through. But once I learned to give myself the right to experience a given emotion and then put it behind me, I began having better days.

• **Walk this way.** If you sense that you're becoming overwhelmed, and you feel your attitude is on the verge of free-fall, take a ten-minute walk and let your brain reset. If you have to rearrange your schedule and make time for this mini-break, then do it. Walk outside, let the sun hit your face, get some fresh air and take some deep breaths before heading back.

• **Find something to laugh about.** We've all heard the saying that laughter is the best medicine, and it is! Laughter allows you to exhale and puts a smile back on your face. When's the last time you got done laughing and felt crappy? Talk to someone in your office that always makes you laugh, or find something on YouTube that makes you smile. The point is, you can turn your day around in a heartbeat by spending a few minutes laughing your troubles away.

Take A Humor Break Right Now!

A husband read an article to his wife about how many words women use a day...8,000 to a man's 4,000. The wife replied, "The reason has to be because a woman has to say everything twice." The husband then turned to his wife and asked, "What?"

• **Use the crystal ball approach.** Focus on what's next instead of what's happened that's turned your mood sour. For some reason, we often dwell on the negative aspects of our day, but if you can put these moments behind you and find something positive to focus on that's coming up, your mood will improve. Good sales people have mastered this tactic, because they know when one prospect tells them "no," they're just one step closer to getting the "yes" they're looking for.

• **Work it out.** And I mean literally go work out. You probably already know this, but when you exercise, your body releases endorphins that can help relieve stress and kick negative energy to the curb. So, hit the stairs, do twenty jumping jacks or take a brisk walk around the block and turn your day around.

• **Pay it forward.** Commit a random act of kindness for someone. This is one of my favorite ways to turn a bad day into a good one. I've paid lunch tabs for the person behind me at a fast-food drive-through, put quarters in expired parking meters and sent flowers (anonymously) to a coworker I knew was going through a rough patch. Opportunities like this are all around you, and if you've never done this before, I encourage you to try it. You'll receive an amazing sensation of satisfaction—and how better to turn things around?

• **Let history work for you.** No matter what's happening or how much your day seems to be getting away from you, you've probably been in a similar situation before that can help you deal with what's going on right now. Pause and remember how you got through a prior experience, and it will help you move forward.

• **Phone a Friend.** Talk to someone who cares about you and knows you well. Sometimes just getting the chance to vent can go a long way at helping you put things in proper perspective and reset your mental state of mind. When venting, be sure to select positive people who will listen and offer support. Negative people tend to breed more negativity, which will only make you feel worse.

• **Count your blessings.** Gratitude has amazing benefits for stress management and personal well-being. And let's face it, if you're focusing on the good things in your life, you can't be paying much attention to what's not going well. Lean back, close your eyes and make a list of the blessings in your life, then let these thoughts take you to your "happy place."

• **Fake it till you make it.** Be aware of your state of mind, and if you find yourself slipping into a hole, you can often stop yourself from going deeper by simply *acting* as if everything is okay. Studies show that although we think that we *act* because of the way we *feel*, in fact, we often *feel* because of the way we *act*.

Talk the Talk

Another critical component to being more positive communicators and increasing the number of good days we have centers around our vocabulary. Studies show that our typical vocabulary has more negative words than positive words, and we seem to spend more time telling people what they *can't* do versus what they *can* do. In fact, children between the ages of six months to three years hear "no" in relation to "yes" in an 80/20 ratio!

There are words that cause negative reactions, and there are positive words that can help set the tone for a conversation. Here are some positive words that you can focus on using more:

Yes • Good • Excellent • Better • Best
Progress * Success * Can & Can-do
Option * Choice * Could * Would
Improved * Enhanced • Possible • Able

And some words to avoid? When looking for ways to incorporate more positive words into your communication style, put these on your hit list:

Can't • Won't • Regret • Unfortunately
Don't • Fail * Deny • Decline * Reject
Impossible • Unable * Difficulty
No • Worst • Should • Inconvenience

Keeping It Positive At Home

Turning cloudy days at work into sunny days is great, but how can you create that same weather pattern when you leave the office and head home? All too often, exhausted couples find a "cold front" waiting for them when they arrive home. Much of the advice I've shared thus far in this chapter applies to relationships with your significant other as well—particularly the section on doling out compliments. Also, I've found that if you work on being a better colleague, coworker and boss, you'll more often than not emerge a better dad and husband or wife and mother.   Here are some other ways to make your romantic life a little warmer and sunnier:

• **Stroll down memory lane.** As relationships mature, we often forget why and what made us fall in love with our partner. We forget the rush we felt from just being with them, how excited we were when we held hands or kissed, or the look in their eyes as we just sat and talked. Laughter, smiles, the pounding of our hearts (and I'm including the guys on this as well) and the anticipation of seeing them again made us feel (legally) high. While we can't recapture those days, we can sure revisit them. I encourage you to set aside some time—at least every other month or so—to reminisce. Pull out photo albums and rehash happy memories. Yeah, I get that life has its demands and responsibilities, but is anything more important than keeping your relationship healthy?

• **Schedule date nights.** I don't care what you do, how crazy your schedules are or what your kids have going on, find times to do something special with your better half. Whether it's a spa night at home, cocktails and appetizers at your favorite bistro, a weekend drive, an impromptu lunch date during the week or a walk around the neighborhood in the evening, each of us has things we enjoy doing together. So, find a reason to go do them.

• **Become fluent in the language of love.** When you get home, walk directly over to your spouse, lean over and whisper something sweet into his/her ear. Tell them how much you love them, how amazing they are to you, how handsome or beautiful they are or how badly you want to get them alone. Use words like, *sensual, sexy, hot, attractive, delicious, excited, aroused* and *gorgeous*. Learn to be a great giver of compliments, and you'll create your own "love potion".

The Magic 5:1 Ratio

In his extensive research of couples, world-renown psychologist John Gottman, Ph.D., found that in stable, happy relationships, couples have a 5:1 ratio between positive interactions and negative interactions. That is, for every criticism and negative comment, there has to be at least 5 compliments and positive comments. The positive interactions build up what Gottman calls "the reservoir of positive feeling". This reservoir is like a savings account into which you are making regular deposits to be withdrawn on a rainy day. Couples who have reservoirs of positive feelings use some of this when they are criticized to offset their hurt feelings so that things balance out. In other words, as long as there are five times as many positive interactions between partners as there are negative, the relationship is likely to be happy and stable.

• **Stay out of "Communication Jail."** This is where couples tend to land when they allow themselves to get too busy to check in and catch up with one another. This lack of regular communication is also the number one cause of arguments and disconnects. So, without the TV on, without the kids vying for your attention and without any other distractions, TALK! I have a saying I often share with my clients: "Twenty minutes of conversation a day will keep the divorce lawyers away." I understand that after a long day, you often just want to relax and "check out," and I'm all in on that. But before you go to bed, you need to "check in" with your significant other. Otherwise, it's far too easy to drift apart.

• **Get your game on.** One of the great benefits of being in a committed relationship is that you can flirt with the person you love. Technology can help you pull this off. Use your smartphone to send text messages or emails. Imagine receiving a text from your partner telling you how much she's looking forward to seeing you when you get home—or even better, what he's going to do to you when you get there. Even a brief "I love you" will go a long way in staying connected. Knowing that the person you've fallen in love with is randomly thinking about you, can be a major turn-on.

Shower the Person You Love With Compliments

"The most important element of romantic passion for both husbands and wives is to feel special. Not only do they want to feel sexually attractive to their mates, but they want to know they are appreciated. Compliments feel good--both to give and to receive. So, to paraphrase a James Taylor song, 'Shower the person you love with compliments.'"

- Les and Leslie Parrott, *Saving Your Marriage Before It Starts*

• **Keep the home fires burning.** With heat and passion, that is. Earlier we talked about taking a walk down memory lane. During that stroll, you may remember how amazing it felt making love when you first met. And how about the frequency with which you connected physically? Early on in most relationships, couples can't seem to get enough of each other. Even brand new sports cars become classics, but that doesn't mean their engines have stopped running; they just don't run as fast as they once did. Make sure you're test driving that car on a regular basis, changing the oil and keeping a fresh set of tires on it. If not, you're at a greater risk of having it break down or drive off one day.

• **Make a joint bucket list.** Put your heads together and brainstorm about things you'd like to do/accomplish as a couple. It can be as simple as a special place you'd like to visit, a new restaurant you've been eager to try out or a new play that's coming to town. And don't forget long-term goals, like taking an exotic vacation, buying a house or starting a business. Making plans together helps both of you stay focused on the future of your relationship.

• **Decompress on the way home.** Learn to leave the "office" behind you and the stress that goes along with it. Listen to some soothing music on the drive home, as music has an amazing power to relax the mind and reduce stress levels. Give yourself a few minutes to decompress and exhale when you first walk in the door. If you've had a tough day, talk about it, but keep the discussion short, since the more you talk about stress, the more stressful you'll become. Besides, if you rehash every annoyance or major problem with your partner every day, you'll start to sound like a chronic complainer.

Overworked? Join the Club!

Now more than ever, it is important that we strive to gain and maintain work-life balance. According to one recent study, 52 percent of employees say that job demands interfere with family or home responsibilities, while 43 percent say that home and family responsibilities interfere with job performance.

Above all, don't let a single day slip by that you don't pause to be thankful for what you have, especially the people in your life who keep you going. We're always hopeful that life has more to offer and that we can improve our material lifestyle, but being appreciative of what you already have (stopping to smell the roses) is critical. Celebrate the love you have daily, and I promise you'll have more sunny days then you can handle.

Chapter Seven

24/7

In previous chapters, I've chronicled the history of communication between men and women, discussed how men and women communicate differently and offered you tools, tips and techniques on how to revolutionize your relationships by becoming a master communicator. This final chapter focuses on *maintaining* the new and improved relationships you've built—which is often easier said than done. That's because maintaining relationships requires time—something we're all short on.

The Great Balancing Act

Quick question: How do you define success at work? According to the latest research, men and women no longer define career success by the size of the paychecks they bring home. In one survey of 50,000 global workers, conducted by the Corporate Executive Board (CEB), work-life balance ranked as one of the most important workplace attributes—second only to compensation. A mere 20 percent of workers polled by the CEB said they valued benefits like on-site gyms or health-care services, while a whopping 60 percent identified flexible schedules as the best benefit their employer could provide.

Results were almost identical in another study conducted by management consulting firm, Accenture. More than half of the 4,100 business executives surveyed cited work-life balance—ahead of money, recognition and autonomy—as the number one determiner of whether or not they had a successful career. In fact, 50 percent had even turned down job offers due to the potential loss of this precious "gift of time."

Give Me a Break!

Employees who feel they have a better work-life balance tend to work 21 percent harder than those that don't.

Is it possible to "have it all?" According to a recent survey, two-thirds of American workers believe that having a successful career *and* a full life outside of work is fully attainable. But is it? In 2006, 53 percent of employees felt they had a good work-life balance. However, a subsequent downturn in the economy—coupled with widespread layoffs and fewer managers and employees left to carry the load—has upended that balance for 31 percent of workers. And when that happens, time with family is the first thing affected, followed by personal down time.

Clearly Not On The Same Page

The fact that nearly 60 percent of Human Resources executives polled felt satisfied with the work-life services of their organization, while just 16 percent of

employees felt the same, illustrates a
fundamental disconnect when it comes to
work-life benefits.

Nowhere To Hide

We can blame technology for most of this imbalance.
With the advent of email, Internet, instant messaging,
laptops, tablets, digital teleconferencing and the like,
our workplaces have changed dramatically over the
last 30 years. On the plus side, these innovations have
changed the way we work, allowing us to be more
productive and accomplish more in less time. On the
down side, they have collapsed the boundaries
between work and home life.

Far too many of us are expected to take our work
load home with us and be on call 24/7 in responding
to emails, texts, phone calls, Skype calls, etc. And
studies show that a whopping two-thirds of us spend
at least some of our vacation time working. Even if
we'd rather not cave into these corporate demands,
most of us feel pressured to do so. "There's an arms-
race component to this," says Lee Rainie, who directs
the Pew Research Center's ongoing study of
technology's social impact. "If someone is sucking up
to the boss at midnight, others think, 'I've got to make
sure I say something, too.'"

Under Pressure

Fathers spend far more time at their jobs
and less time on housework and childcare
than mothers, according to a new Pew
Research Center study, which dissects
results of the U.S. government's American
Time Use Survey. The study also found
that mothers spend around 32 hours per

week on childcare and housework, compared to fathers' 17 hours. Meanwhile, mothers average 21 hours per week on paid work, compared to 37 hours for fathers. The survey shows that 50 percent of working dads and 56 percent of working moms report that it is "very" or "somewhat" difficult to balance family and work responsibilities.

Screen Time Vs. Face Time

Of course, many of us *choose* to remain plugged in at home—texting, tweeting, checking out Facebook statuses, chatting online and playing games with friends on our smartphones. But being always connected can take a huge toll on our relationships by robbing us of the personal communication that bonds us to others. *First For Women* magazine recently called upon my expertise to help out John and Sarah, a couple whose eight-year marriage was in trouble. "As social as my wife is, I don't understand why she can't give me a little attention every now and then," John complained. "I don't get why I have to fight for equal time with her gadgets."

Countered Sarah, "John seems to think I *want* to run myself ragged 24/7. After a long day at work, I handle most of the cooking and cleaning, then to unwind, I'll usually check emails, Facebook or make a few calls. When he sees me do this, he'll usually mumble something, then disappear into his workshop."

Over time, I got Sarah to work on powering down. She agreed to a two-hour block of tech-free time each night and gave John her undivided attention. Once their evenings were spent reconnecting, John and Sarah got back to the fundamental emotions and goose bump moments they felt in the beginning of their marriage.

Virtually every time you turn an electronic device *on*, you're likely tuning out someone you care about *out*...including your children.

In her blog, *Hands Free Mama*, which looks at how to use technology in a mindful way, Rachel Macy Stafford shares some sobering thoughts she received from youngsters when she brought up the topic of turning off devices and interacting with loved ones. Among the verbatim responses: "My dad has a problem putting down his phone." "My mom texts and drives." "Sometimes I say something, and my dad doesn't hear me because he is typing on his phone." Stafford said she didn't want to judge the behaviors of others but noted that "the children's remarks indicate there is a disturbing problem in our society."

Waiting To Exhale

I'm going to date myself a little here, but I remember when I was a kid, the world seemed to pause each week to take a deep breath and rejuvenate before starting a brand new week. Sundays were a day of rest and devoted to spending time with family. Very few businesses were open, and the ones that were operated on an abbreviated schedule. You couldn't run to the mall and go shopping or even fill up your car with gas. Sundays were sacred—a day to exhale, spend time with family and friends and just "be." That meant having the opportunity to recharge your batteries, connect with loved ones and enjoy some quality down time.

In today's environment, Wal-Mart is open 24/7, and Sundays are more about getting done what you didn't have time to accomplish on Saturday. Not surprisingly, insufficient down time not only has the potential to wreck your relationships, it can also jeopardize your health. When you don't get enough sleep or take time to exercise or engage in activities you love (golf, tennis, socializing with family and friends), it's impossible to keep your body and mind healthy and sharp.

Disconnect to Connect

Staying balanced at work and at home is critical to maintaining strong, healthy relationships with coworkers and loved ones. But finding that balance may involve going through digital detox. In 2010, the nonprofit, Reboot, declared a specific day in March as a National Day of Unplugging. The group encouraged gadget users to turn off their devices for 24 hours and reclaim some personal time—and the idea caught on big time. I encourage you to try to carve out one or two days a week (even half days will suffice) for unplugging, unwinding, relaxing, reflecting, getting outdoors and, above all, reconnecting with loved ones.

Building Better, Stronger Relationships

"Relationships are like cars in that you have to do certain things to keep them running." Love this quote from Brian Ogolsky, Ph.D., Professor of Human and Community Development at the University of Illinois. Revolutionizing your relationships definitely requires upkeep, but it's not as difficult as it sounds and offers huge benefits. At work—regardless of your rank or tenure—collegiality and camaraderie are the "grease" that make day-to-day operations run smoothly and efficiently. Not to mention that in today's workplace— where a team-based mentality prevails—how well you get along with those you work with can determine your *own* professional success. In fact, studies show that effective working relationships form the basis for promotion, pay increases, goal accomplishment, and job satisfaction. So, take a little extra time and effort to:

• **Dig a little deeper.** Show a genuine interest in your coworkers by asking them about their families, hobbies, passions, and what's going on in their lives outside of work. Then, make mental notes about what you learn and be prepared to ask follow up questions ("How did the barbecue fundraiser go on Sunday?" "Did your daughter's soccer team win last night?") or extend best wishes ("Happy anniversary!" or "Have a blast at the concert this weekend!"). When appropriate, talk about your own life outside the office as well. This leads others to believe you care about them, which in turn, makes them feel more comfortable around you. It also enables staffers to appreciate each other as people, not merely colleagues.

• **Solicit their input.** Who doesn't love being asked to share their thoughts or opinions about something? Maybe you need a second pair of eyes to look over a project summary, or you could use some unbiased advice about how to handle a sticky situation with a client. Even if you don't agree with what others offer, asking for their two cents is flattering and makes them feel valued and important.

• **Avoid office politics.** Unfortunately, workplaces can be a lot like high school. Aside from cliques and drama, there are always folks who spend a whole lot of time spreading rumors, backstabbing, sucking up and trying to take credit for others' ideas. Having constructive conversations about coworkers is fine, but walk away from the gossip and negativity. If you don't, people won't trust you—and, worse, they'll wonder what you're saying about them behind their back.

• **Share credit.** When you get props for an accomplishment or an idea, chances are you didn't act alone. Always take the time to thank, reward and recognize the contributions of those who help you succeed. This is a no-fail approach to building rock-solid work relationships.

• **Have their back.** When Kerry Patterson, coauthor of the New York Times bestseller *Crucial Conversations*, conducted focus groups and asked folks to name the most important characteristics of a valued coworker, the one phrase he repeatedly heard was, "someone who has my back." "They said the best coworkers are those who are there when they need someone to pitch in and those who defend them in their absence," Patterson notes. "These employees can be counted on to be advocates and work in their coworker's best interest."

• **Be a teacher/mentor.** Studies show that sharing your skills and knowledge with coworkers increases your status as a leader. It also solidifies your reputation as a team player. And perhaps more importantly, it endears you to others as someone who's invested in their success.

• **Be a person of your word.** If someone trusts you to honor a deadline or a commitment and you flake out on them—poof, that trust is gone. If you're not able to complete your work on time—and hey, it happens—give others who are depending on you a heads up as quickly as possible. Don't make excuses ("I've got a lot of personal stuff going on") or pass blame (e.g., "Cheryl didn't give me the data I needed on time"), but do present a solid plan to make things right. Also, make a habit of returning phone calls and emails in a timely manner. Nobody likes being ignored, and everybody likes having his or her concerns addressed as quickly as possible. Lengthy delays make others feel unimportant.

• **Lend a hand.** When you have free time and notice a coworker who is swamped and overwhelmed, offer to pitch in and help him/her meet a deadline. The effort and generosity behind gestures like this go a long way in creating a bond. Ask for help when you need it, too.

By admitting that you also rely on the support of others to get things done, you establish a foundation on which you can build respect—a key ingredient for good relationships.

• **Touch base frequently.** After a project or an assignment ends, stay in touch with folks you've enjoyed working with. Invite them to lunch or cocktails after work. Shoot them a quick email or text to ask what's up. Or send an article you think they might find interesting. These are simple but very powerful ways to cultivate positive working relationships.

Keeping It Real At Home

What about maintaining your relationships at home? There's a tendency for couples in committed relationships to get comfortable with each other, which is something we all crave. But studies show that too much comfort causes boredom and tension, which can lead to drifting apart instead of growing closer together. Fortunately, there are many ways to superglue the relationship you have with your significant other and continue connecting on a deeper level—even years into your partnership. Here's what I recommend:

• **Get real.** Don't be afraid to be vulnerable (guys, are you listening?). Connecting with your significant other when your life is going great is easy, but showing your more vulnerable side by talking about topics that intimidate or frighten you can be a challenge. The good news is, there's an upside to being vulnerable. When you let your defenses down, your partner sees the real you, allowing your significant other to join in and experience what's going on with you mentally. Not to mention what an amazingly freeing experience it can be when you're not afraid to be exactly who you are with someone you trust and love.

It takes courage to let your guard down, but I urge you to strive for full disclosure—of the good, the bad, and the ugly. I promise you that the personal payoffs will be huge! Getting "naked" emotionally enables you to get to know—and trust—each other to the very core. And once everything is out in the open, you can work together to help and support each other, which can intensify your emotional connection. Perhaps best of all, being able to share your needs, hopes, and fears leaves you with that amazing feeling that there's at least one person on the planet that totally "gets" you.

• **Commit random acts of affection.** I'm talking about an unsolicited hug or a random kiss on the cheek. We talked about the amazing benefits of touch earlier in this book, but it bears repeating: Few things are as good for the soul and the emotional health of a person—and for your relationship—as human touch. Feeling the hands of your loved one wrap around your waist from behind can be a powerful moment. How about brushing your hand across your partner's backside as you pass by? That can be a fun, playful moment. Or, how about leaning over to whisper in your partner's ear, "I love you" when he/she least expects it? These actions don't take a great deal of effort, but they can go a long way in communicating how special the love of your life is to you and helping the two of you reconnect on a regular basis.

• **Schedule relationship check ups:** We go to the doctor for routine physicals, and we visit the dentist for annual check-ups, so why not conduct routine relationship check-ups? This is a fantastic opportunity to touch base with your partner and get a feel for how they're doing and how they're feeling about the direction of your relationship. Schedule a time when the two of you can sit down in a calm setting with no distractions, and take turns sharing how you feel about work, home, the kids or any other topic that comes to mind. Not sure where to start? I always encourage the couples I work with to ask the following three questions:

What can I do differently to make you happy and cause you to want to sprint home at the end of the day?

How can I show you how much I love you?

How are we doing in the bedroom?

Honest answers to these questions can have a tremendous impact on your relationship, because you'll discover if your individual needs are being met—and if they're not, you can put your heads together and figure out how to make that happen. By taking an inventory of what is and isn't working in your relationship, you get a jump-start on resolving small, solvable issues before they turn into big, unsolvable ones.

Keep Talking

(Even When Your Mouth Is Full!)

Here's what researchers studying the conversational patterns of thousands of couples during the dinner hour recently discovered:

• While dating, couples converse for 50 minutes out of a 60-minute hour. The couple only spends ten minutes actually eating. No wonder a meal during a date takes so long!

Immediately after marriage, the time spent talking begins to slowly shrink:

- After twenty years of marriage, the average time spent talking drops to 21 minutes out of the hour.

- Thirty years into a marriage, the couple spends only 16 minutes talking.

- The 50-year marriage mark sees the average couple talking for only three minutes during a meal hour.

- **Divide and conquer.** Studies say women report higher levels of work-family conflict than do men— mostly because they still devote more hours per week than men do to childcare and household chores. But the levels of work-life conflict reported by men are increasing. I highly recommend sharing the workload at home and, whenever possible, try blasting some music you both love and working together to knock out your to-do list. That way, not only will your chores get finished faster, you'll have more time to plan something fun to do together.

The Kids Will Be Alright

If you have children and you both work, you know how much parenting responsibilities can limit one-on-one couple time. Studies of dual-earner families show that parents' needs and satisfactions tend to take a "back seat" to the demands and needs of their children. From caring for their youngsters and cheering them on from the sidelines of whatever extracurricular activity they're participating in, to helping with homework and playing games, parents typically allow the kids' needs and desires to dictate their own schedules. But while spending time together as a family is important, it is equally important to spend time together as a couple. So, make a conscious effort to set aside time each day or make weekly "dates" to connect.

• **Don't be so predictable.** Consistency is nice and all—and routines are a necessity to keep our lives and households running smoothly—but don't get too comfortable. It can be quite stimulating for yourself, as well as your relationship, to be more spontaneous and explore beyond your comfort zone. Make a play date with your significant other and do something different, adventure out to a new place or try a new activity together. Any time you mix up your routine is a bonding opportunity.

Find ways to spice up your sex life, too. Make love in unusual places or experiment with new positions, toys or products. And share fantasies. Research reveals that nine out of ten of us have them—and the tenth person probably has them, too, but just won't admit it. What's more, couples that share fantasies make love more often—so start the dialogue!

MEET COACH TODD REED, CPC

Todd Reed is Certified Professional Coach and a four-time, award-winning Broadcaster of the Year who boasts nearly two decades of interpersonal coaching and on-air television and radio experience. From calling the shots as a sports anchor to hosting morning drive time segments and live call-in shows, he has covered the gamut. But The Coach's true passion and greatest area of expertise lies in Communication & Relationships.

That passion led him to write his first book, *Conversation is Sexy*, an Amazon.com bestseller that offers tips, tools, and techniques for couples in committed relationships on how to discover/rediscover the joys of being in love.

Coach Todd has recently been a guest on CBS, NBC and FOX affiliates. He has appeared on over 75 radio shows coast-to-coast and been invited to host a nationally syndicated radio talk show. He has also been featured as a relationship expert in national and international publications, including *Woman's World*, *Men's Health Singapore* and *First for Women.*

Coach Todd specializes in giving keynote speeches, leading seminars, and providing consulting/coaching services in the areas of communication and relationships. For more information on these services, contact:

Todd Reed, CPC
(406) 396-7755 or (706) 255-9301
coachtoddreed@gmail.com * www.coachtoddreed.com

REFERENCES

Abercromby, M. "A report on the importance of work-life balance." Retrieved from: http://www.bia.ca/articles/AReportontheImportanceofWork-Life Balance.htm

"An 8th grader who is far more honest with his girlfriend than you are." Retrieved from: http://www.happyplace.com/20831/eighth-graders-love-note-way-more-honest-than-youll-ever-be-with-a-significant-other

Blackwelder, J.K. *Now Hiring: The Feminization of Work in the United States, 1900–1995.* Texas: Texas A&M University Press, 1997.

Breslin, S. "How to work for a female boss." Retrieved from: http://www.forbes.com/sites/susanahbreslin/2012/06/27/female-boss-tips/

Brooks, C. "Career success means work-life balance, study finds," Retrieved from: http://www.huffingtonpost.com/2013/03/05/career-success-means-work-life-balance_n_2812707.html

Brounstein, M. "Business coaching: Using constructive feedback vs. praise and criticism. Retrieved from: http://www.dummies.com/how-to/content/business-coaching-using-constructive-feedback-vers.html

Byron. E. "A truce in the chore wars, cleaning brands retool." Retrieved from: http://www.prsresearch.com/prs-insights/article/a-truce-in-the-chore-wars-cleaning-brands-retool/

Callahan, M. "7 ways to keep work stress out of your relationship." Retrieved from http://www.huffingtonpost.com/dr-michelle-callahan/tips-for-managing-work-stress_b_1000290.html

Clark, L. "Building a strong marriage – finding time." Retrieved from: http://ohioline.osu.edu/flm02/FS02.html

Engel, B. "The power of apology." Retrieved from:
http://www.psychologytoday.com/articles/200208/the-power-apology

Flora, C. "Make a great impression." Retrieved from:
http://www.psychologytoday.com/articles/200407/make-great-impression

Glaser, C. and B.S. Smalley. *Swim With the Dolphins: How Women Can Succeed in Corporate America On Their Own Terms.* New York: Warner Books, 1995.

Glaser, C. *GenderTalk Works (If You Do It Right): 7 Steps for Cracking the Gender Code at Work.* New York: Windsor Hall Press, 2007.

Glaser, C. and B. Smalley. *When Money Isn't Enough: How Women Are Finding the Soul of Success.* New York: Warner Books, 1999.

Goudreau, J. "The 10 worst stereotypes about powerful women." Retrieved from:
http://www.forbes.com/sites/jennagoudreau/2011/10/24/worst-stereotypes-powerful-women-christine-lagarde-hillary-clinton/

Goman, C.K. "10 simple and powerful body language tips for 2013." Retrieved from:
http://www.forbes.com/sites/carolkinseygoman/2013/01/07/10-simple-and-powerful-body-language-tips-for-2013/

Gray, J. *Mars and Venus in the Workplace: A Practical Guide for Improving Communication and Getting Results at Work.* New York: HarperCollins, 2002.

Manion, J. *From Management to Leadership: Strategies for Transforming Health.* San Francisco: Josey-Bass, 2011.

Newport, F. "Americans still prefer male bosses; many have no preference." Retrieved from:
http://www.gallup.com/poll/149360/americans-prefer-male-bosses-no-preference.aspx

Nixon, R. "10 things every man should know about a woman's brain." Retrieved from: http://www.livescience.com/14421-human-brain-gender-differences.html

Orman, M., M.D. ""7 keys to listening that will win you friends, improve your marriage, boost your profits, and make people want to follow you anywhere!" Retrieved from: http://www.stresscure.com/relation/7keys.html

Patterson, K., J. Grenny, R. McMillan and A. Switzler. *Crucial Conversations: Tools for Talking When Stakes Are High.* New York: McGraw Hill, 2011.

Pease, B. and A. Pease. *Why Men Don't Listen and Women Can't Read Maps: How We're Different and What to Do About It.* New York: Welcome Rain Publishers, 2000.

Pease, A. and B. Pease. *Why Men Lie and Women Cry.* London: Orion, 2002.

Petrecca, L. "All work and no play? Mobile wipes out 8-hour workday." Retrieved from: http://www.usatoday.com/story/news/nation/2013/03/06/mobile-workforce-all-work/1958673/

Petrecca, L. "Always on? How to switch off in a digital world." Retrieved from: http://www.usatoday.com/story/news/nation/2013/03/06/mobile-devices-how-to-switch-off-and-unplug/1969537/

Ponder, C. "6 tips on making it through a difficult conversation with your boss." Retrieved from: http://www.blogging4jobs.com/hr/6-tips-on-making-it-through-a-difficult-conversation-with-your-boss/

Radwan, M.F. "Psychological differences between men and women. Retrieved from: http://www.2knowmyself.com/psychological_differences_between_men_and_women

Rath, T. and D.O. Clifton. "The big impact of small interactions." Retrieved from: http://businessjournal.gallup.com/content/12916/big-impact-small-interactions.aspx

Roberts, K. "Neuroimage study finds scientific reasoning why men have trouble listening to women." Retrieved from:

http://www.abcactionnews.com/dpp/lifestyle/neuroimage-study-finds scientific-reasoning-why-men-have-trouble-listening-to women#ixzz2Sdxj2v30

Robinson, B. "The power of positive communications." Retrieved from: http://www.scribd.com/doc/120009175/The-Power-of-Positive-Communications

Rubin, G. "The power of praise." Retrieved from: http://www.webmd.com/balance/features/the-power-of-praise

Scher, H. "Do you complain too much? (or not enough?)." Retrieved from: http://www.webmd.com/balance/features/do-you-complain-too-much

"Stress and women." Retrieved from: http://my.clevelandclinic.org/healthy_living/stress_management/hic_stress_and_women.aspx

Strobel, M. *The Compliment Quotient: Boost Your Spirits, Spark Your Relationships and Uplift the World.* Littleton, CO: Wise Roads Press, 2011.

Taibbi, R. "How to talk to a man; how to talk to a woman." Retrieved from: http://www.psychologytoday.com/blog/fixing-families/201211/how-talk-man-how-talk-woman

"The increasing call for work-life balance." Retrieved from: http://www.businessweek.com/managing/content/mar2009/ca20090327_734197.htm

"The magic 5:1 ratio." Retrieved from: http://behavioralhealth.typepad.com/markhams_behavioral_healt/2004/05/the_magic_51_ra.html

U.S. Department of Labor Statistics. http://www.bls.gov/

"Women in Business." Retrieved from: http://www.referenceforbusiness.com/encyclopedia/Val-Z/Women-in-Business.html#ixzz2Nr3gheb3

WHAT CLIENTS ARE SAYING
ABOUT TODD REED, CPC

"You are a charismatic and dynamic speaker with a real gift for connecting with people. Your tips and advice are refreshing and memorable, but what makes you such a joy to listen to is your keen sense of humor. Keep up the great work and come back soon!"
- *Robert Veroulis, Fellowship of Christian Athletes*

"A million thanks for your excellent program! Our sales and marketing staff is still buzzing about you and all the creative ideas you shard with them. It was a home run!"
- *Mallory Lopp, The Lopp Agency, Inc.*

"You were outstanding! Insightful, relevant, entertaining, and on target. Encore! Encore!"
- *Barbara Smalley, Desktop Creations, Inc.*

"I used your tips and techniques to grow my small business, and in less than two years, despite tough economic times, my company's revenues have tripled!"
- *Eleanor Thompson, Cincinnati, OH*

"Thanks for speaking at our campus-wide fraternity and sorority event. You shared some eye opening information, and your delivery was off the charts. It's unanimous: we're ready to book you for a return visit!"
- *Bobby Cockerille, Virginia Commonwealth University*

"When the company I work for started laying folks off, I thought for sure I would be getting a pink slip. But my boss told me my customer service skills were way too valuable to let me go. I learned most of what I know from you, Coach. Thanks so much!"
- *Natalie Simpson, Tampa, FL*

Todd Reed, CPC
(406) 396-7755 or (706) 255-9301
coachtoddreed@gmail.com * www.coachtoddreed.com

Made in the USA
Lexington, KY
12 November 2015